ASSASSIN'S CREED®

VALHALLA

FORGOTTEN MYTHS

ASSASSIN'S CREED

VALHALLA

FORGOTTEN MYTHS

ALEXANDER FREED // SCRIPT

MARTÍN TÚNICA // ART

MICHAEL ATIYEH // COLORS

JIMMY BETANCOURT OF COMICRAFT // LETTERS

RAFAEL SARMENTO // COVERS

DARK HORSE BOOKS

MIKE RICHARDSON // PRESIDENT AND PUBLISHER

SPENCER CUSHING // EDITOR

KONNER KNUDSEN // ASSISTANT EDITOR

SARAH TERRY // DESIGNER

MATT DRYER // DIGITAL ART TECHNICIAN

SPECIAL THANKS TO ALEX HARAKIS, PIERRE BOUDREAU, LOUIS BARRAUD, FATIHA CHELLALI, AND CAROLINE LAMACHE AT UBISOFT.

ASSASSIN'S CREED© VALHALLA: FORGOTTEN MYTHS

This volume collects the Dark Horse comic book series *Assassin's Creed Valhalla: Forgotten Myths* #1–#3.

Published by Dark Horse Books
A division of Dark Horse Comics LLC
10956 SE Main Street // Milwaukie, OR 97222

DarkHorse.com

First edition: September 2022
Ebook ISBN 978-1-50672-976-3 // ISBN 978-1-50672-975-6

10 9 8 7 6 5 4 3 2 1
Printed in China

MIX
Paper from responsible sources
FSC® C169962
FSC www.fsc.org

Library of Congress Cataloging-in-Publication Data

Names: Freed, Alexander, author. | Túnica, Martín, artist. | Atiyeh, Michael, colorist. | Betancourt, Jimmy, letterer. | Sarmento, Rafael, cover artist.
Title: Assassin's creed valhalla : forgotten myths / script by Alexander M. Freed ; art by Martin Tunica ; colors by Michael Atiyeh ; letters by Jimmy Betancourt of Comicraft ; covers by Rafael Sarmento.
Description: First edition. | Milwaukie, OR : Dark Horse Books, 2022. | "This volume collects the Dark Horse comic books Assassin's Creed Valhalla: Forgotten Myths #1-4." | Summary: "War is about to break out between the two neighboring realms of Muspelheim and Svartalfheim. Surtr, lord of the Muspels, is gathering his army of fire giants. Determined to prevent such bloodshed, Baldr, son of Odin and god of light, enlists the help of the great trickster god, Loki"-- Provided by publisher.
Identifiers: LCCN 2022014601 (print) | LCCN 2022014602 (ebook) | ISBN 9781506729756 (hardcover) | ISBN 9781506729763 (ebook)
Subjects: LCGFT: Fantasy comics. | Graphic novels.
Classification: LCC PN6728.A768 F74 2022 (print) | LCC PN6728.A768 (ebook) | DDC 741.5/973--dc23/eng/20220407
LC record available at https://lccn.loc.gov/2022014601
LC ebook record available at https://lccn.loc.gov/2022014602

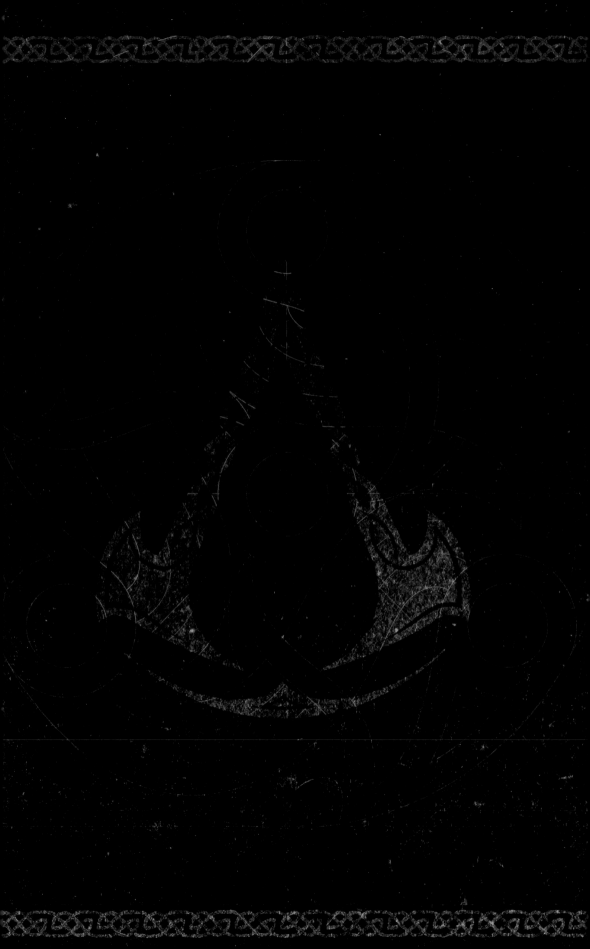

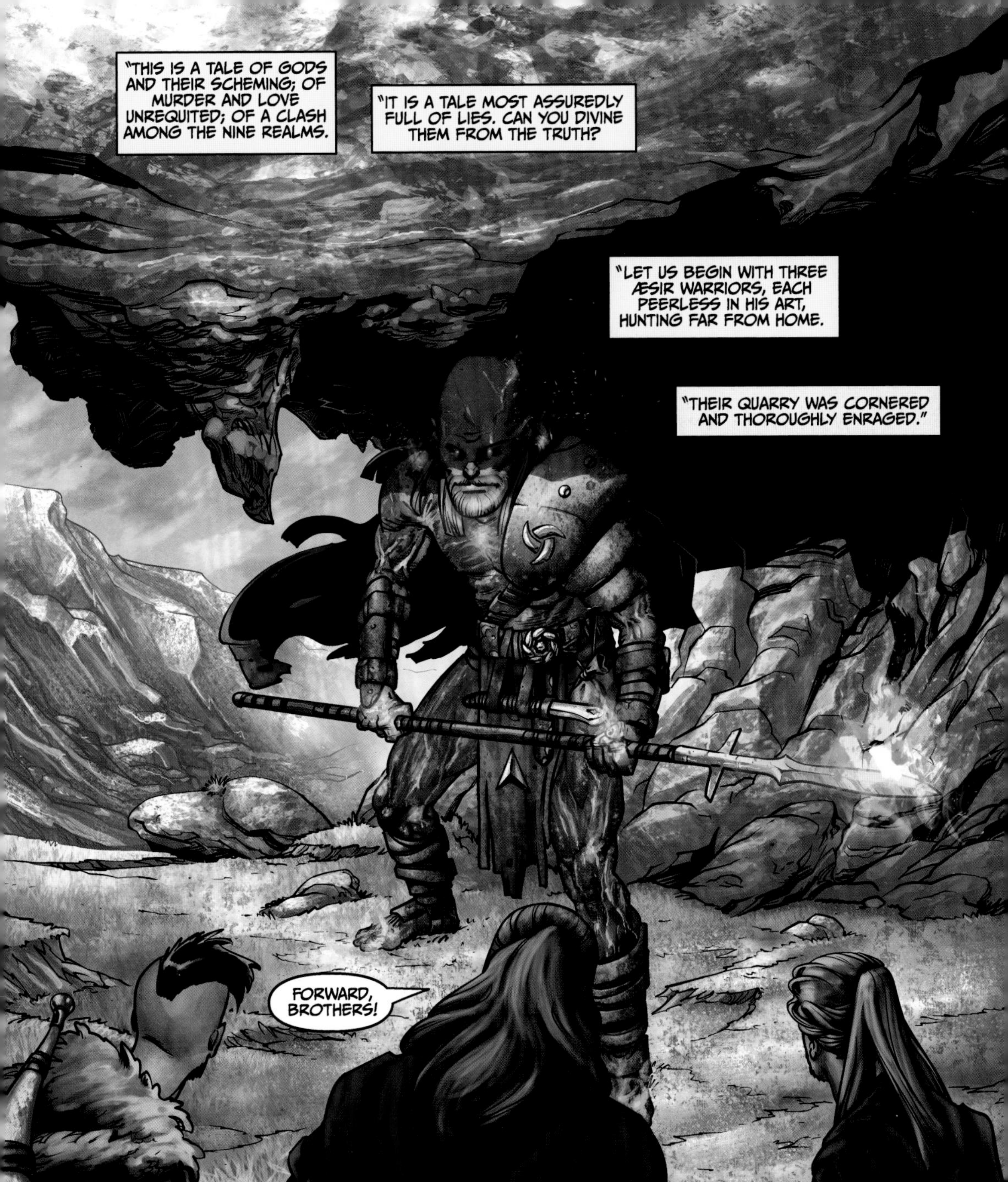
"THIS IS A TALE OF GODS AND THEIR SCHEMING; OF MURDER AND LOVE UNREQUITED; OF A CLASH AMONG THE NINE REALMS.
"IT IS A TALE MOST ASSUREDLY FULL OF LIES. CAN YOU DIVINE THEM FROM THE TRUTH?
"LET US BEGIN WITH THREE ÆSIR WARRIORS, EACH PEERLESS IN HIS ART, HUNTING FAR FROM HOME.
"THEIR QUARRY WAS CORNERED AND THOROUGHLY ENRAGED."
FORWARD, BROTHERS!

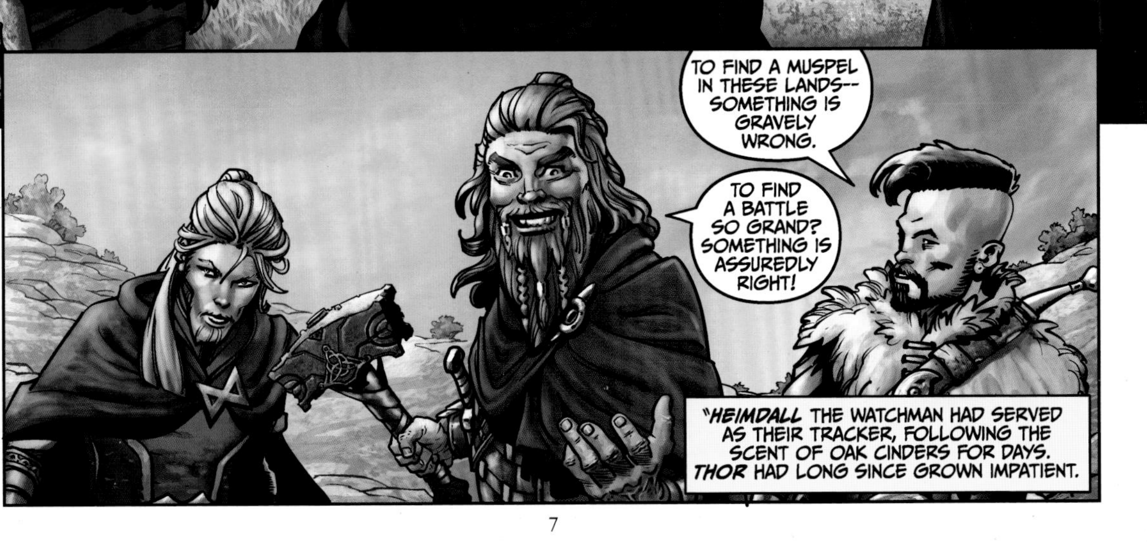
TO FIND A MUSPEL IN THESE LANDS-- SOMETHING IS GRAVELY WRONG.
TO FIND A BATTLE SO GRAND? SOMETHING IS ASSUREDLY RIGHT!
"HEIMDALL THE WATCHMAN HAD SERVED AS THEIR TRACKER, FOLLOWING THE SCENT OF OAK CINDERS FOR DAYS. THOR HAD LONG SINCE GROWN IMPATIENT.

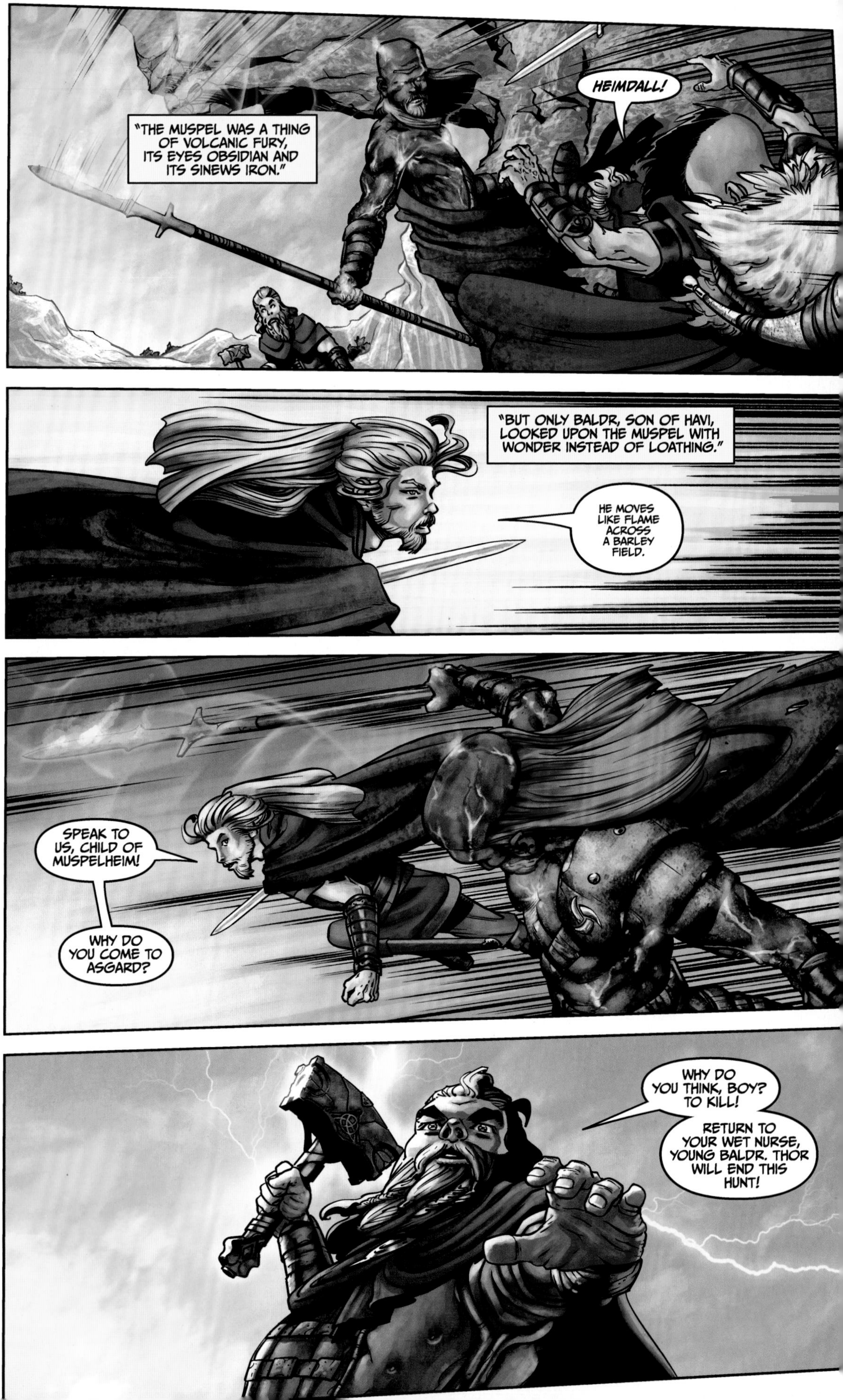
"THE MUSPEL WAS A THING OF VOLCANIC FURY, ITS EYES OBSIDIAN AND ITS SINEWS IRON."
HEIMDALL!
"BUT ONLY BALDR, SON OF HAVI, LOOKED UPON THE MUSPEL WITH WONDER INSTEAD OF LOATHING."
HE MOVES LIKE FLAME ACROSS A BARLEY FIELD.
SPEAK TO US, CHILD OF MUSPELHEIM!
WHY DO YOU COME TO ASGARD?
WHY DO YOU THINK, BOY? TO KILL!
RETURN TO YOUR WET NURSE, YOUNG BALDR. THOR WILL END THIS HUNT!

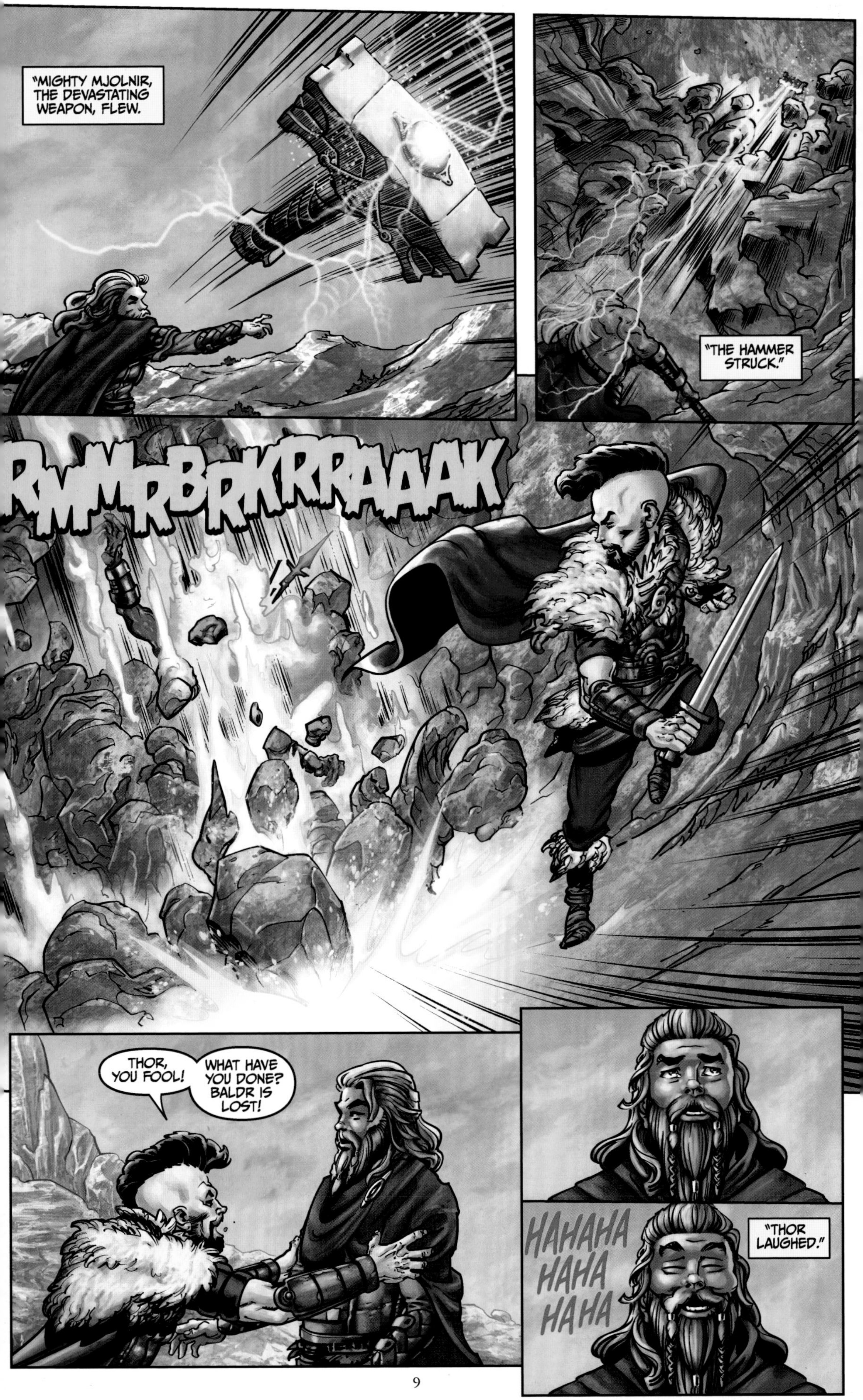
"MIGHTY MJOLNIR, THE DEVASTATING WEAPON, FLEW.
"THE HAMMER STRUCK."
RMMRBRKRRAAAK
THOR, YOU FOOL!
WHAT HAVE YOU DONE? BALDR IS LOST!
HAHAHA HAHA HAHA
"THOR LAUGHED."

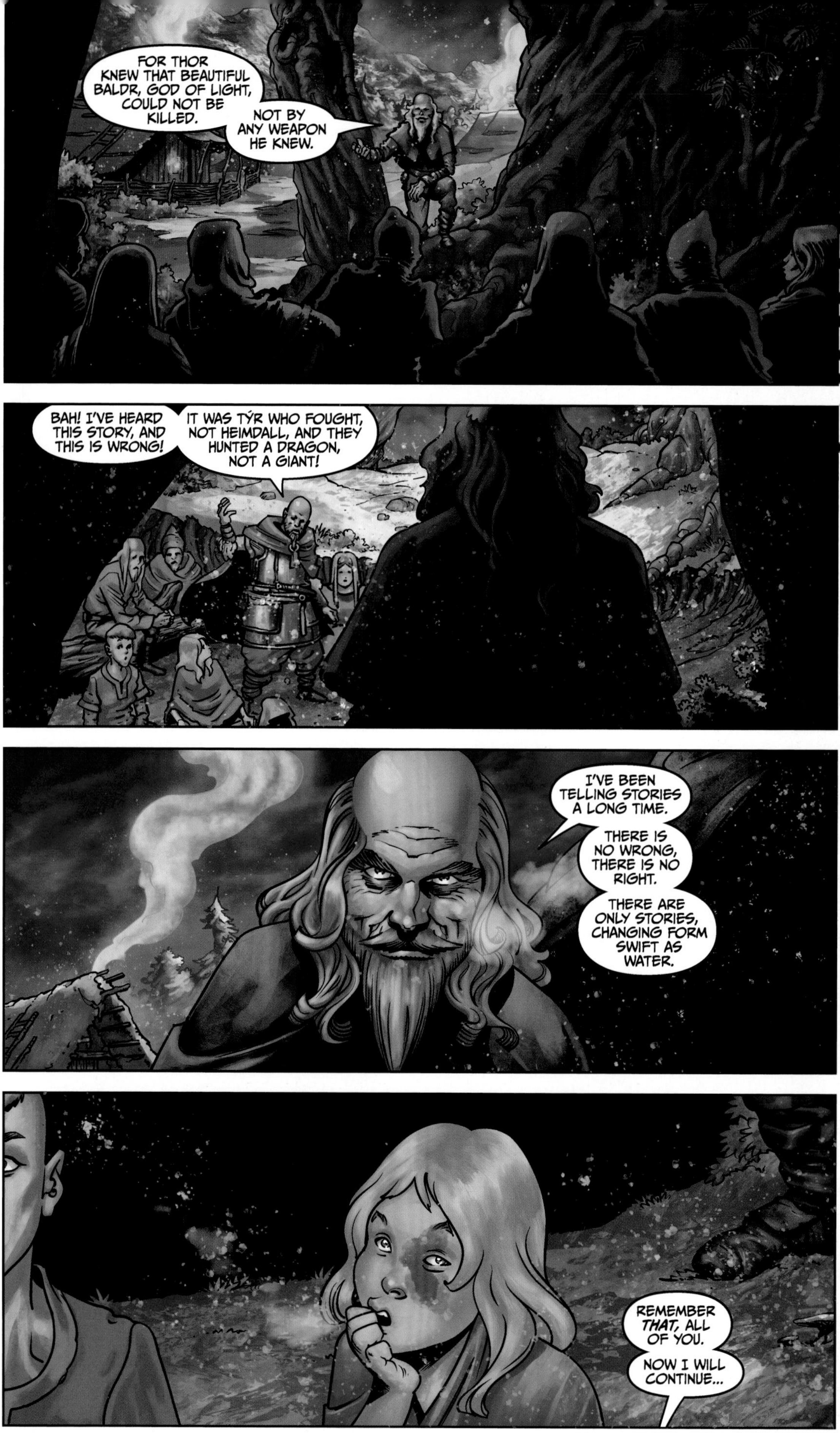
FOR THOR KNEW THAT BEAUTIFUL BALDR, GOD OF LIGHT, COULD NOT BE KILLED.
NOT BY ANY WEAPON HE KNEW.
BAH! I'VE HEARD THIS STORY, AND THIS IS WRONG!
IT WAS TÝR WHO FOUGHT, NOT HEIMDALL, AND THEY HUNTED A DRAGON, NOT A GIANT!
I'VE BEEN TELLING STORIES A LONG TIME.
THERE IS NO WRONG, THERE IS NO RIGHT.
THERE ARE ONLY STORIES, CHANGING FORM SWIFT AS WATER.
REMEMBER *THAT*, ALL OF YOU.
NOW I WILL CONTINUE...

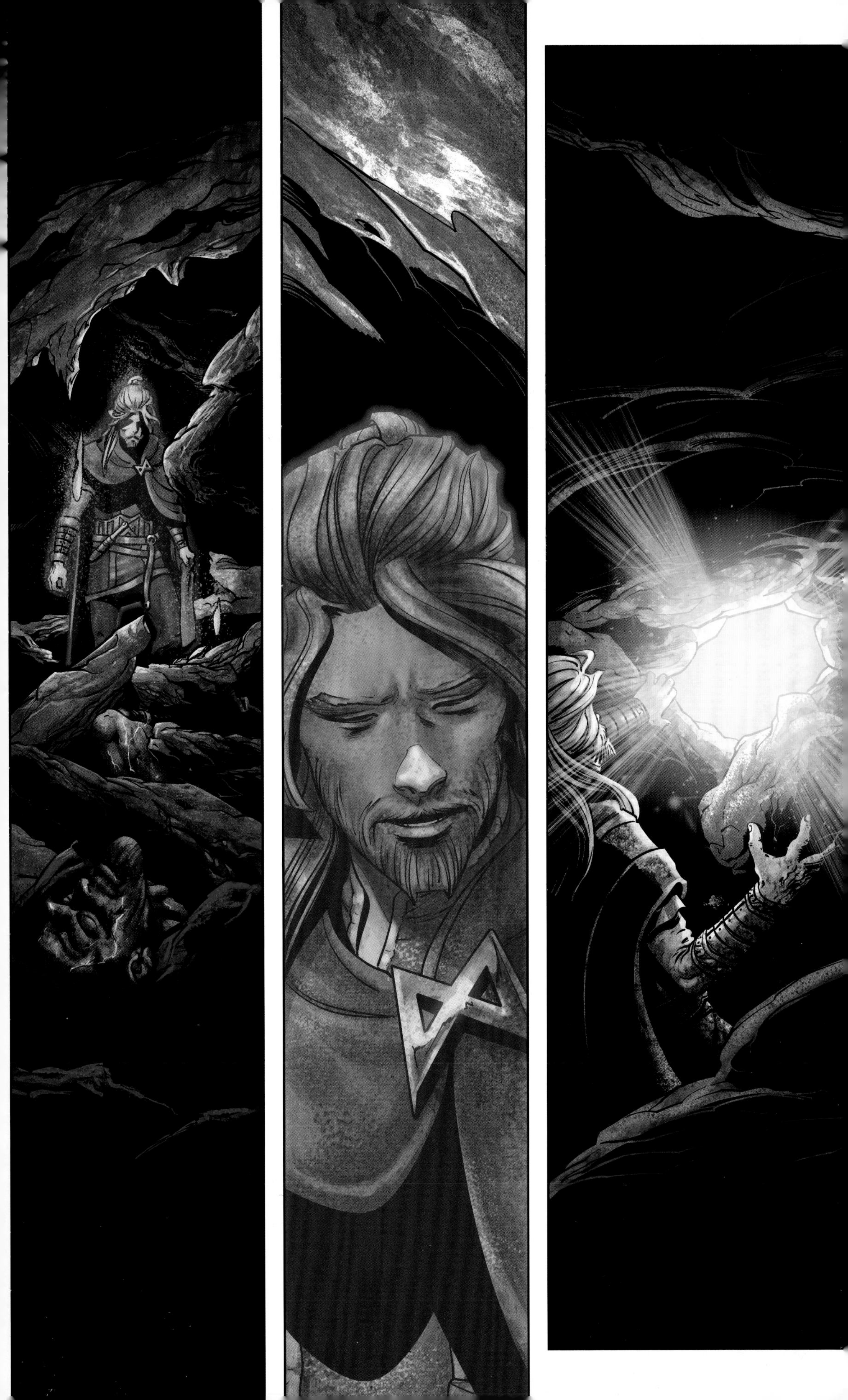

"MOVING STONES ONE BY ONE, HE OPENED GAPS AND TWISTED THROUGH NARROW SPACES, ARRIVING IN BARELY WIDER TUNNELS.

"THERE, HE SAW A FLAME."

HELLO?

RAISE NO WEAPONS AND DO NO HARM.

GLADLY, ELDER DWARF.

WHO ARE YOU?

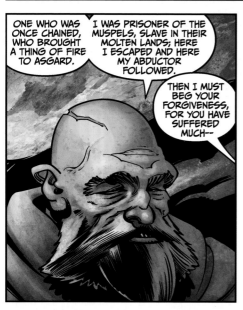

ONE WHO WAS ONCE CHAINED, WHO BROUGHT A THING OF FIRE TO ASGARD.

I WAS PRISONER OF THE MUSPELS, SLAVE IN THEIR MOLTEN LANDS; HERE I ESCAPED AND HERE MY ABDUCTOR FOLLOWED.

THEN I MUST BEG YOUR FORGIVENESS, FOR YOU HAVE SUFFERED MUCH--

--AND NOW YOU ARE TRAPPED, THANKS TO THE CLUMSINESS OF OUR HUNT.

I PROMISE YOU HOSPITALITY, GOLD, JEWELS WHEN WE REACH THE SURFACE--

≈PFFT!≈

DWARVES ARE DIGGERS BY NATURE, UNLIKE GANGLY ÆSIR.

FREEDOM IS NOT FAR, AND NEEDS NO PAYMENT.

"THEY MARCHED AND CRAWLED THROUGH VAST AND NARROW SPACES, THE DWARF FLINGING GREAT STONES AS THE CAVERN ROOF GROANED."

HOW DID YOU COME TO BE PRISONER OF THE MUSPELS?

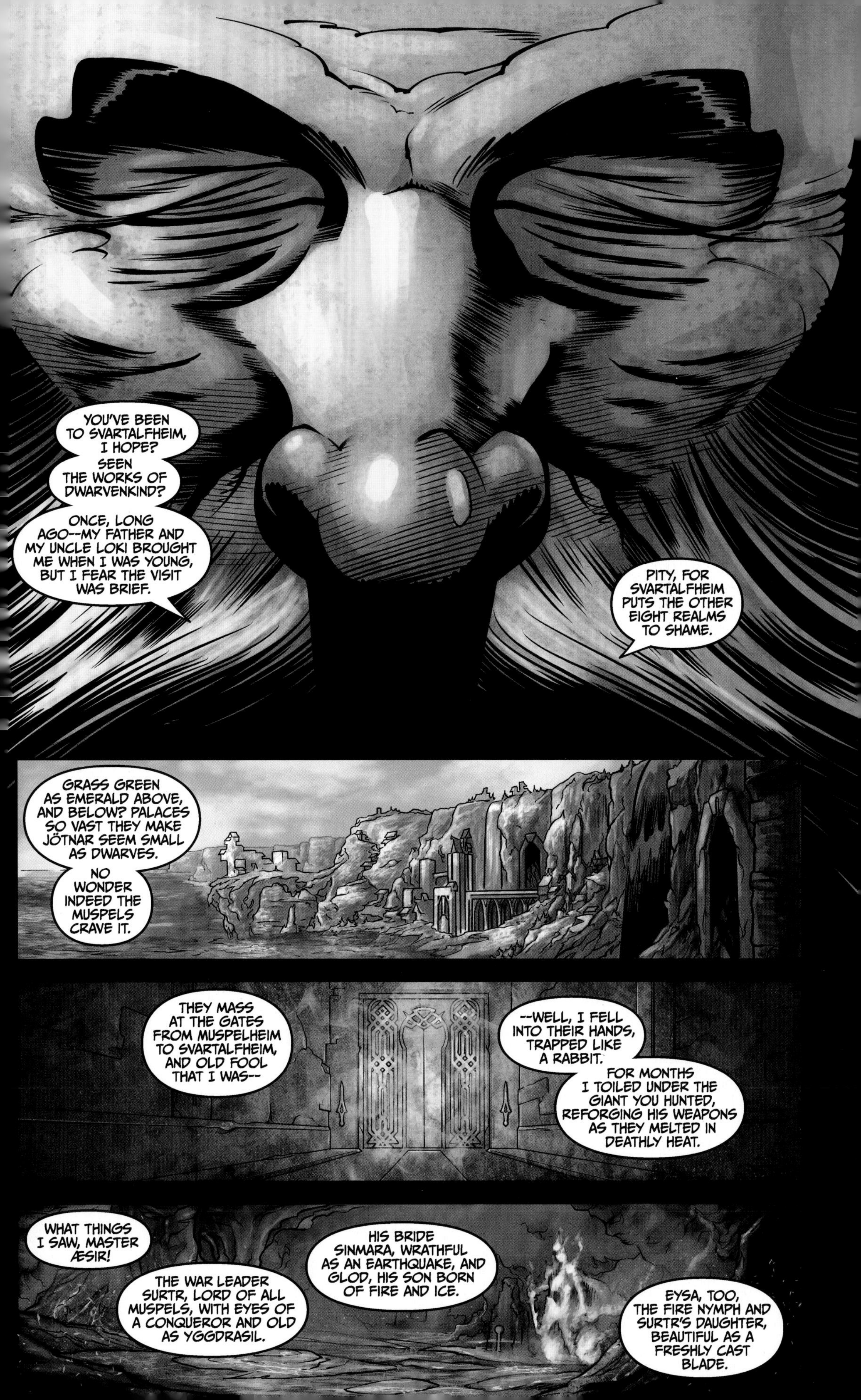
YOU'VE BEEN TO SVARTALFHEIM, I HOPE?
SEEN THE WORKS OF DWARVENKIND?
ONCE, LONG AGO--MY FATHER AND MY UNCLE LOKI BROUGHT ME WHEN I WAS YOUNG, BUT I FEAR THE VISIT WAS BRIEF.
PITY, FOR SVARTALFHEIM PUTS THE OTHER EIGHT REALMS TO SHAME.
GRASS GREEN AS EMERALD ABOVE, AND BELOW? PALACES SO VAST THEY MAKE JÖTNAR SEEM SMALL AS DWARVES.
NO WONDER INDEED THE MUSPELS CRAVE IT.
THEY MASS AT THE GATES FROM MUSPELHEIM TO SVARTALFHEIM, AND OLD FOOL THAT I WAS--
--WELL, I FELL INTO THEIR HANDS, TRAPPED LIKE A RABBIT.
FOR MONTHS I TOILED UNDER THE GIANT YOU HUNTED, REFORGING HIS WEAPONS AS THEY MELTED IN DEATHLY HEAT.
WHAT THINGS I SAW, MASTER ÆSIR!
THE WAR LEADER SURTR, LORD OF ALL MUSPELS, WITH EYES OF A CONQUEROR AND OLD AS YGGDRASIL.
HIS BRIDE SINMARA, WRATHFUL AS AN EARTHQUAKE, AND GLOD, HIS SON BORN OF FIRE AND ICE.
EYSA, TOO, THE FIRE NYMPH AND SURTR'S DAUGHTER, BEAUTIFUL AS A FRESHLY CAST BLADE.

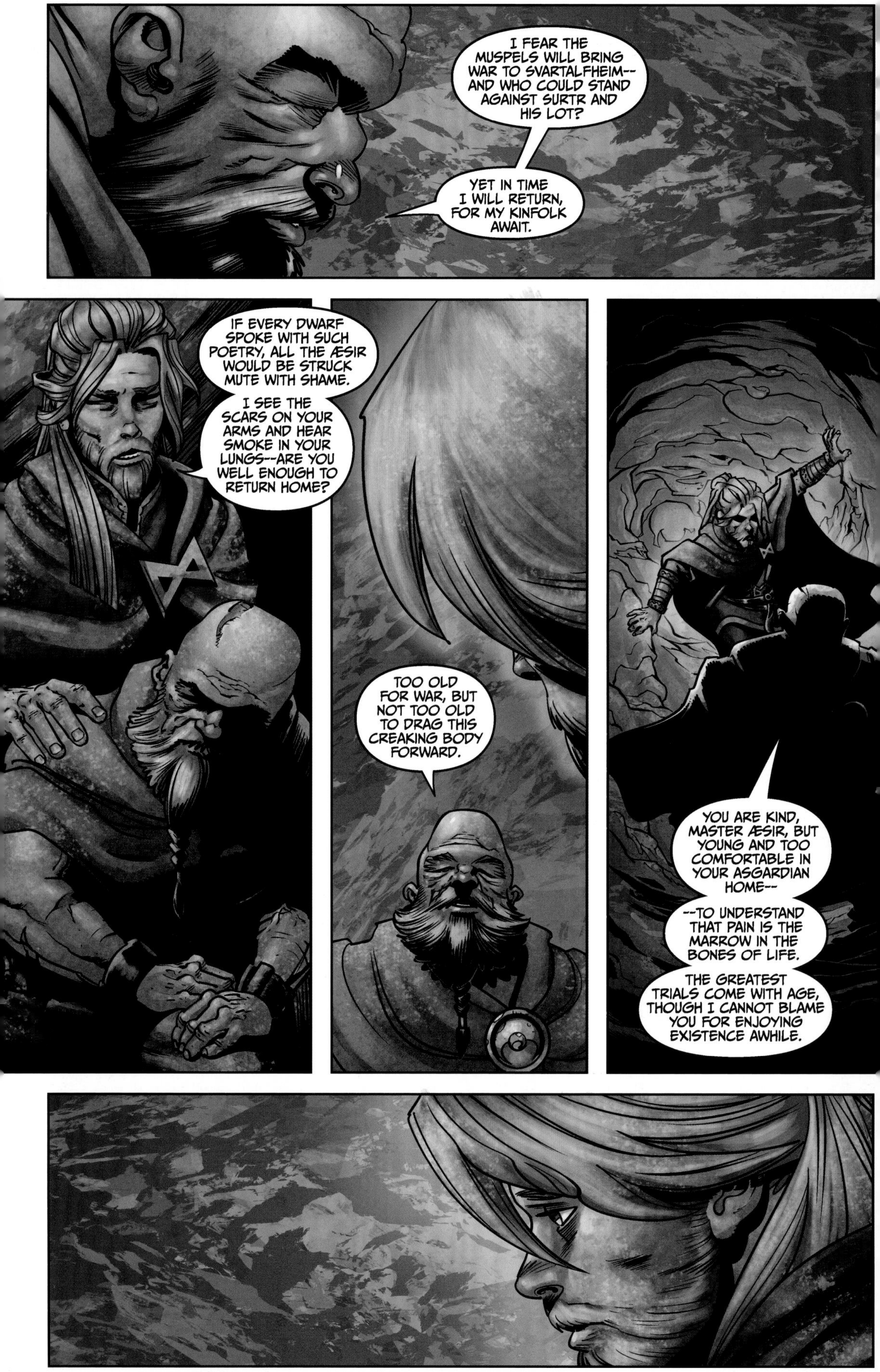
I FEAR THE MUSPELS WILL BRING WAR TO SVARTALFHEIM-- AND WHO COULD STAND AGAINST SURTR AND HIS LOT?
YET IN TIME I WILL RETURN, FOR MY KINFOLK AWAIT.
IF EVERY DWARF SPOKE WITH SUCH POETRY, ALL THE ÆSIR WOULD BE STRUCK MUTE WITH SHAME.
I SEE THE SCARS ON YOUR ARMS AND HEAR SMOKE IN YOUR LUNGS--ARE YOU WELL ENOUGH TO RETURN HOME?
TOO OLD FOR WAR, BUT NOT TOO OLD TO DRAG THIS CREAKING BODY FORWARD.
YOU ARE KIND, MASTER ÆSIR, BUT YOUNG AND TOO COMFORTABLE IN YOUR ASGARDIAN HOME--
--TO UNDERSTAND THAT PAIN IS THE MARROW IN THE BONES OF LIFE.
THE GREATEST TRIALS COME WITH AGE, THOUGH I CANNOT BLAME YOU FOR ENJOYING EXISTENCE AWHILE.

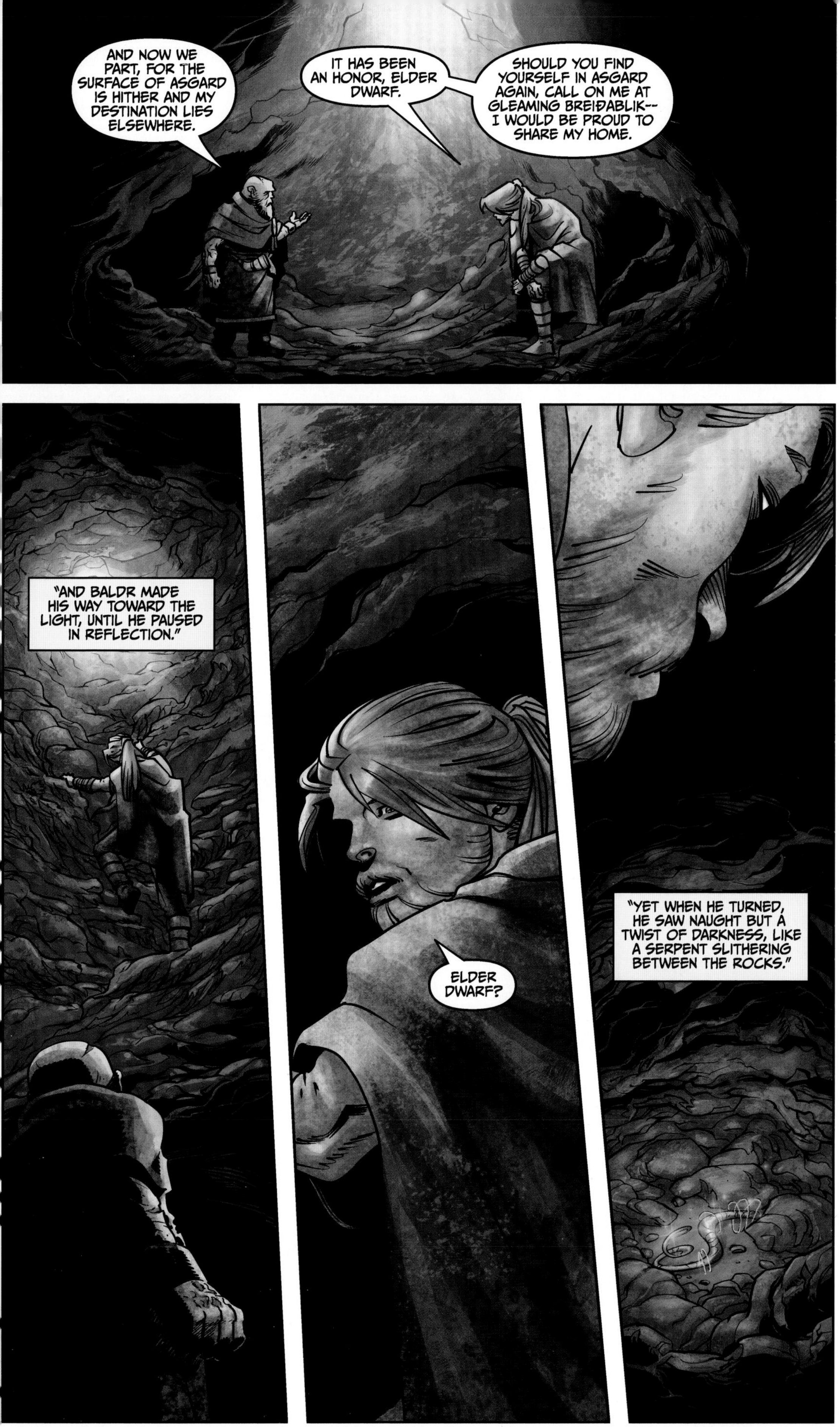
AND NOW WE PART, FOR THE SURFACE OF ASGARD IS HITHER AND MY DESTINATION LIES ELSEWHERE.
IT HAS BEEN AN HONOR, ELDER DWARF.
SHOULD YOU FIND YOURSELF IN ASGARD AGAIN, CALL ON ME AT GLEAMING BREIÐABLIK-- I WOULD BE PROUD TO SHARE MY HOME.
"AND BALDR MADE HIS WAY TOWARD THE LIGHT, UNTIL HE PAUSED IN REFLECTION."
ELDER DWARF?
"YET WHEN HE TURNED, HE SAW NAUGHT BUT A TWIST OF DARKNESS, LIKE A SERPENT SLITHERING BETWEEN THE ROCKS."

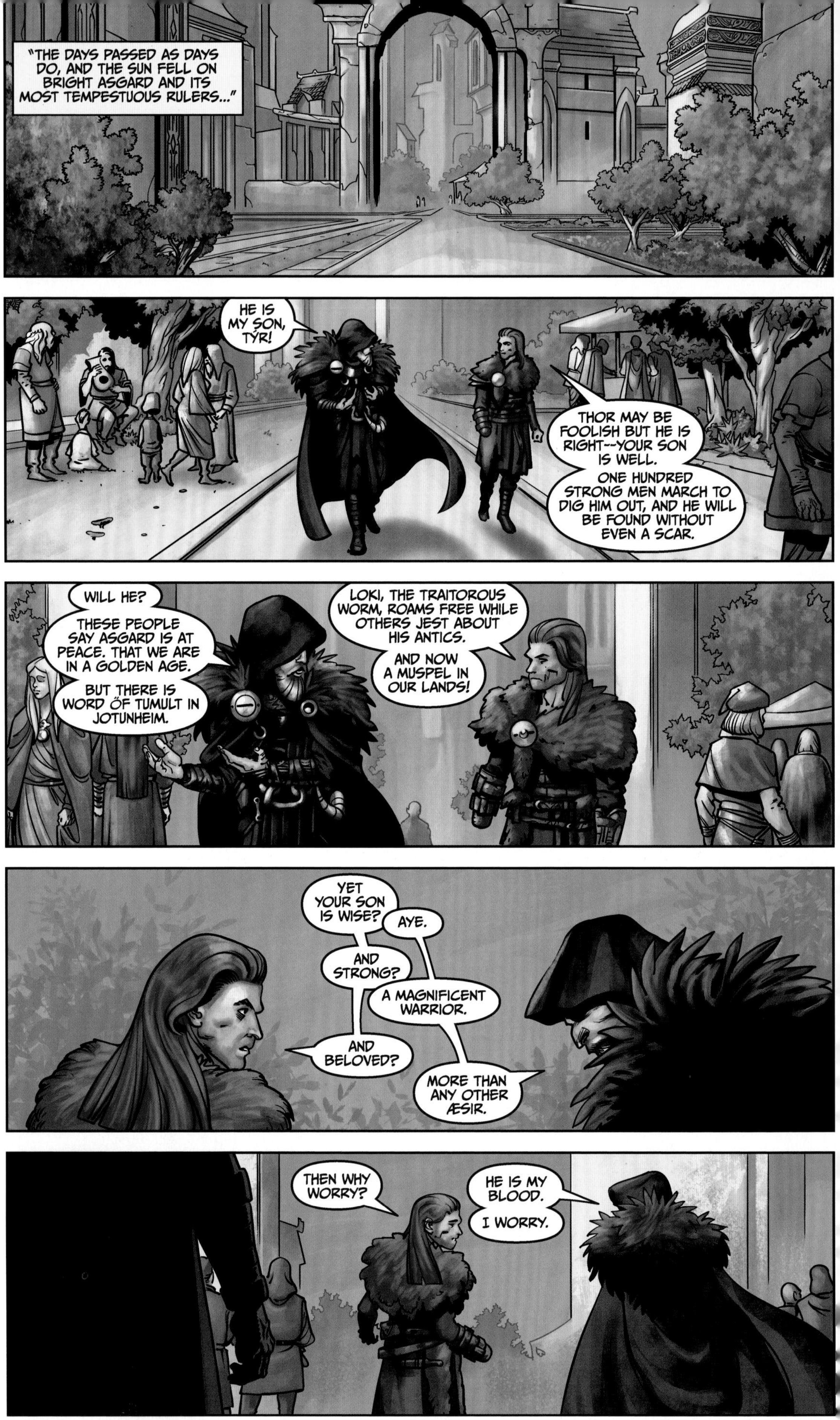
"THE DAYS PASSED AS DAYS DO, AND THE SUN FELL ON BRIGHT ASGARD AND ITS MOST TEMPESTUOUS RULERS..."
HE IS MY SON, TYR!
THOR MAY BE FOOLISH BUT HE IS RIGHT--YOUR SON IS WELL.
ONE HUNDRED STRONG MEN MARCH TO DIG HIM OUT, AND HE WILL BE FOUND WITHOUT EVEN A SCAR.
WILL HE?
THESE PEOPLE SAY ASGARD IS AT PEACE. THAT WE ARE IN A GOLDEN AGE.
BUT THERE IS WORD ÖF TUMULT IN JOTUNHEIM.
LOKI, THE TRAITOROUS WORM, ROAMS FREE WHILE OTHERS JEST ABOUT HIS ANTICS.
AND NOW A MUSPEL IN OUR LANDS!
YET YOUR SON IS WISE?
AYE.
AND STRONG?
A MAGNIFICENT WARRIOR.
AND BELOVED?
MORE THAN ANY OTHER ÆSIR.
THEN WHY WORRY?
HE IS MY BLOOD.
I WORRY.

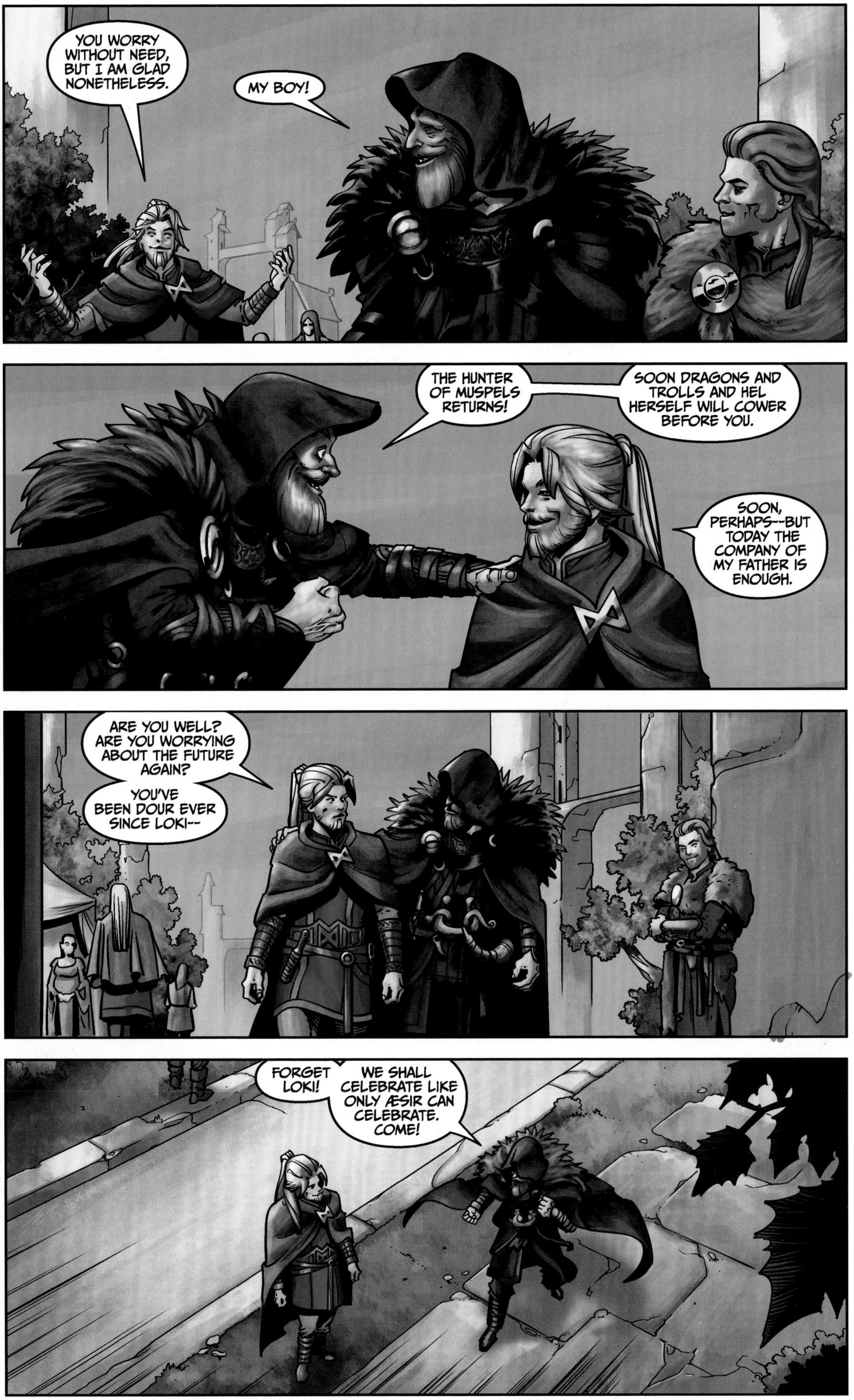
YOU WORRY WITHOUT NEED, BUT I AM GLAD NONETHELESS.
MY BOY!
THE HUNTER OF MUSPELS RETURNS!
SOON DRAGONS AND TROLLS AND HEL HERSELF WILL COWER BEFORE YOU.
SOON, PERHAPS--BUT TODAY THE COMPANY OF MY FATHER IS ENOUGH.
ARE YOU WELL? ARE YOU WORRYING ABOUT THE FUTURE AGAIN?
YOU'VE BEEN DOUR EVER SINCE LOKI--
FORGET LOKI!
WE SHALL CELEBRATE LIKE ONLY ÆSIR CAN CELEBRATE. COME!

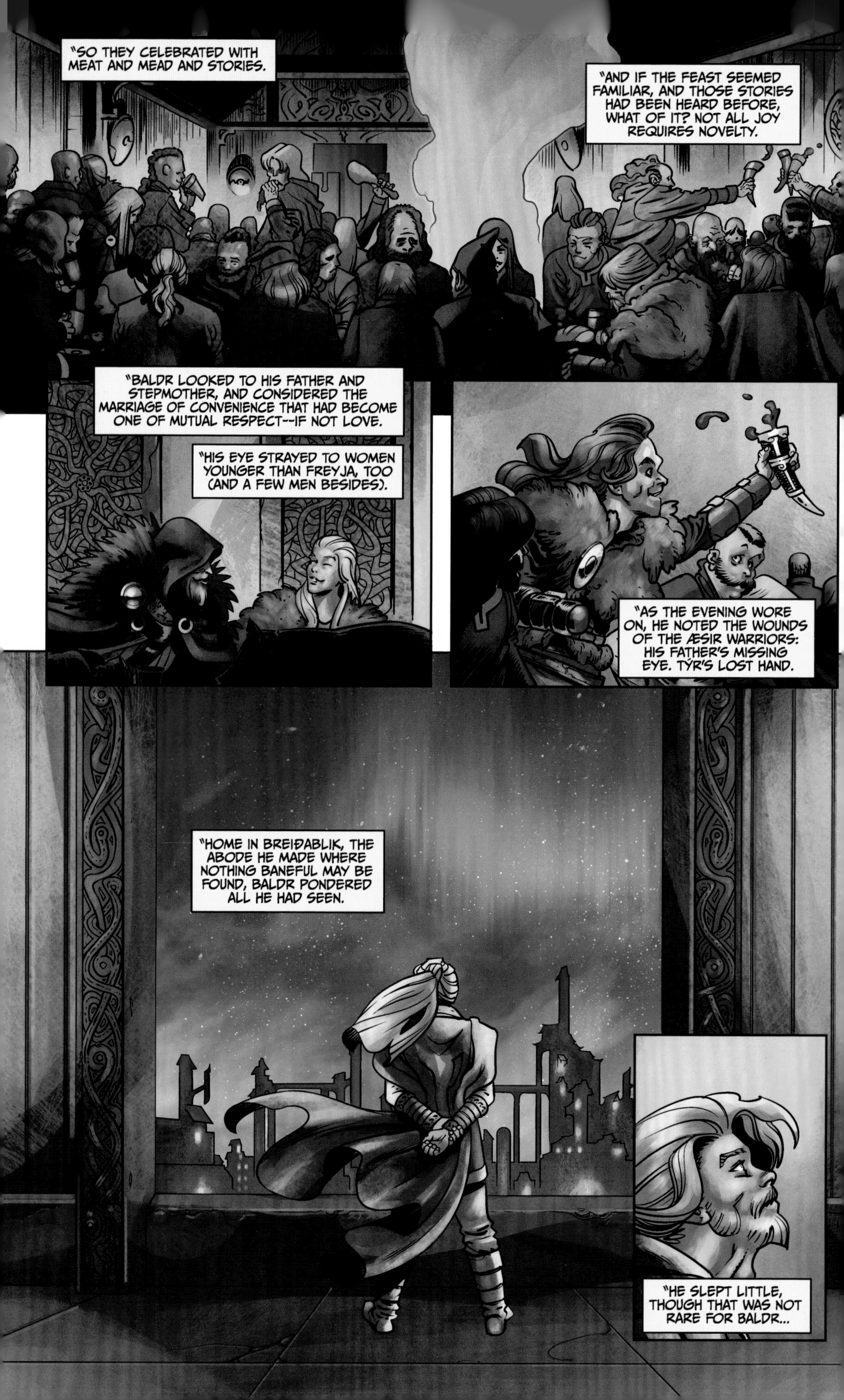
"SO THEY CELEBRATED WITH MEAT AND MEAD AND STORIES.
"AND IF THE FEAST SEEMED FAMILIAR, AND THOSE STORIES HAD BEEN HEARD BEFORE, WHAT OF IT? NOT ALL JOY REQUIRES NOVELTY.
"BALDR LOOKED TO HIS FATHER AND STEPMOTHER, AND CONSIDERED THE MARRIAGE OF CONVENIENCE THAT HAD BECOME ONE OF MUTUAL RESPECT--IF NOT LOVE.
"HIS EYE STRAYED TO WOMEN YOUNGER THAN FREYJA, TOO (AND A FEW MEN BESIDES).
"AS THE EVENING WORE ON, HE NOTED THE WOUNDS OF THE ÆSIR WARRIORS: HIS FATHER'S MISSING EYE. TÝR'S LOST HAND.
"HOME IN BREIÐABLIK, THE ABODE HE MADE WHERE NOTHING BANEFUL MAY BE FOUND, BALDR PONDERED ALL HE HAD SEEN.
"HE SLEPT LITTLE, THOUGH THAT WAS NOT RARE FOR BALDR...

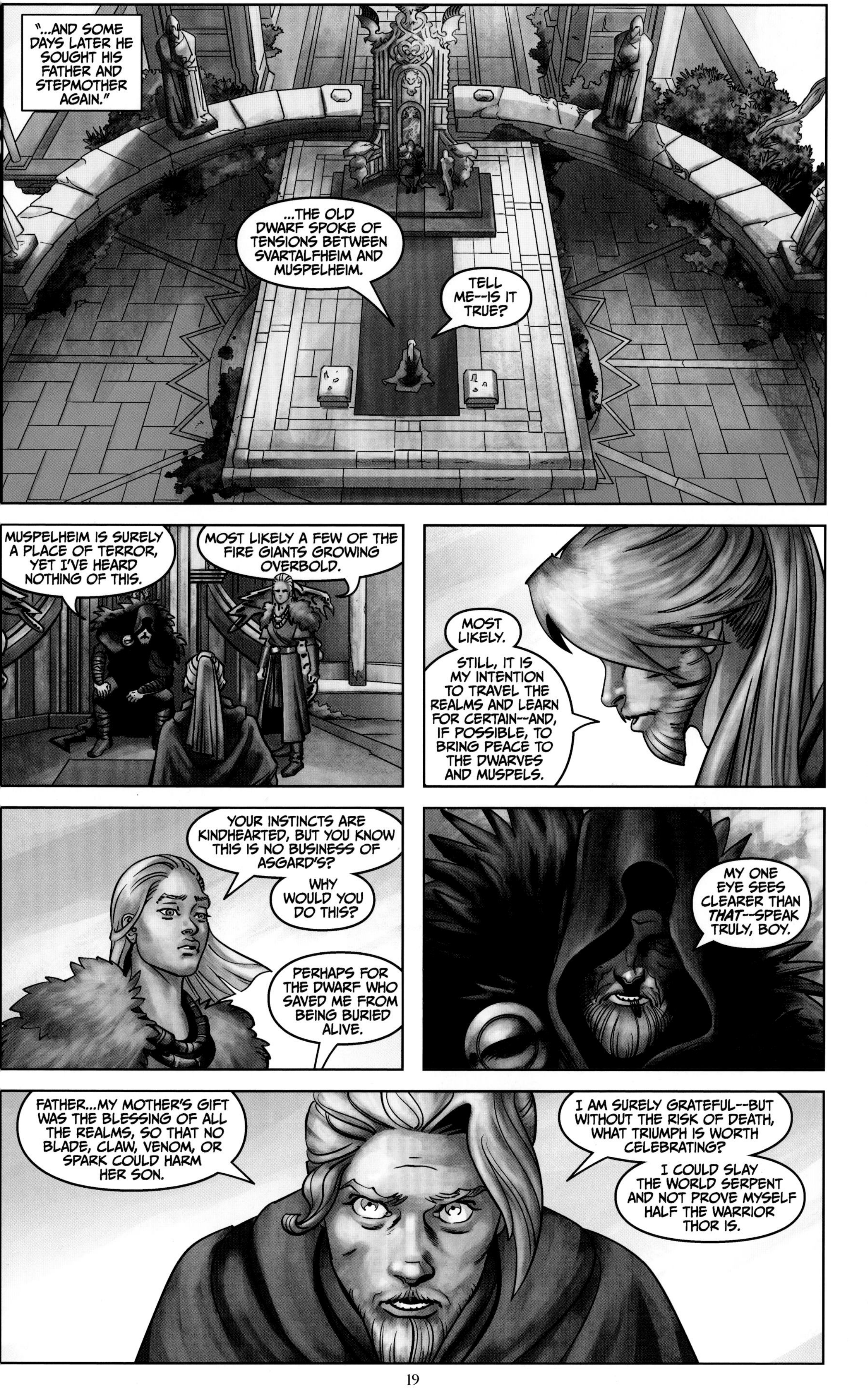
"...AND SOME DAYS LATER HE SOUGHT HIS FATHER AND STEPMOTHER AGAIN."
...THE OLD DWARF SPOKE OF TENSIONS BETWEEN SVARTALFHEIM AND MUSPELHEIM.
TELL ME--IS IT TRUE?
MUSPELHEIM IS SURELY A PLACE OF TERROR, YET I'VE HEARD NOTHING OF THIS.
MOST LIKELY A FEW OF THE FIRE GIANTS GROWING OVERBOLD.
MOST LIKELY.
STILL, IT IS MY INTENTION TO TRAVEL THE REALMS AND LEARN FOR CERTAIN--AND, IF POSSIBLE, TO BRING PEACE TO THE DWARVES AND MUSPELS.
YOUR INSTINCTS ARE KINDHEARTED, BUT YOU KNOW THIS IS NO BUSINESS OF ASGARD'S?
WHY WOULD YOU DO THIS?
PERHAPS FOR THE DWARF WHO SAVED ME FROM BEING BURIED ALIVE.
MY ONE EYE SEES CLEARER THAN THAT--SPEAK TRULY, BOY.
FATHER...MY MOTHER'S GIFT WAS THE BLESSING OF ALL THE REALMS, SO THAT NO BLADE, CLAW, VENOM, OR SPARK COULD HARM HER SON.
I AM SURELY GRATEFUL--BUT WITHOUT THE RISK OF DEATH, WHAT TRIUMPH IS WORTH CELEBRATING?
I COULD SLAY THE WORLD SERPENT AND NOT PROVE MYSELF HALF THE WARRIOR THOR IS.

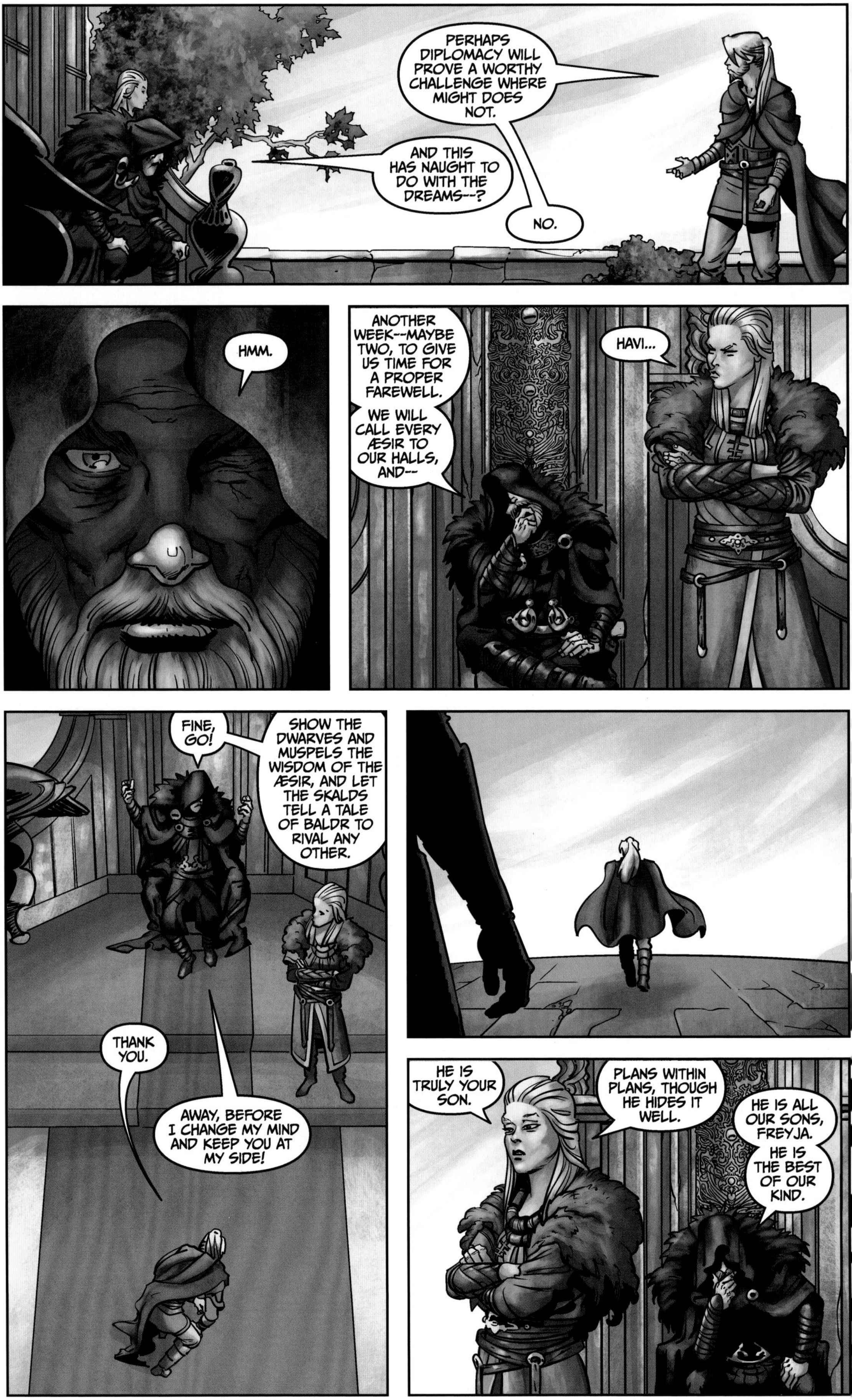

PERHAPS DIPLOMACY WILL PROVE A WORTHY CHALLENGE WHERE MIGHT DOES NOT.
AND THIS HAS NAUGHT TO DO WITH THE DREAMS--?
NO.
HMM.
ANOTHER WEEK--MAYBE TWO, TO GIVE US TIME FOR A PROPER FAREWELL.
WE WILL CALL EVERY ÆSIR TO OUR HALLS, AND--
HAVI...
FINE, GO!
SHOW THE DWARVES AND MUSPELS THE WISDOM OF THE ÆSIR, AND LET THE SKALDS TELL A TALE OF BALDR TO RIVAL ANY OTHER.
THANK YOU.
AWAY, BEFORE I CHANGE MY MIND AND KEEP YOU AT MY SIDE!
HE IS TRULY YOUR SON.
PLANS WITHIN PLANS, THOUGH HE HIDES IT WELL.
HE IS ALL OUR SONS, FREYJA.
HE IS THE BEST OF OUR KIND.

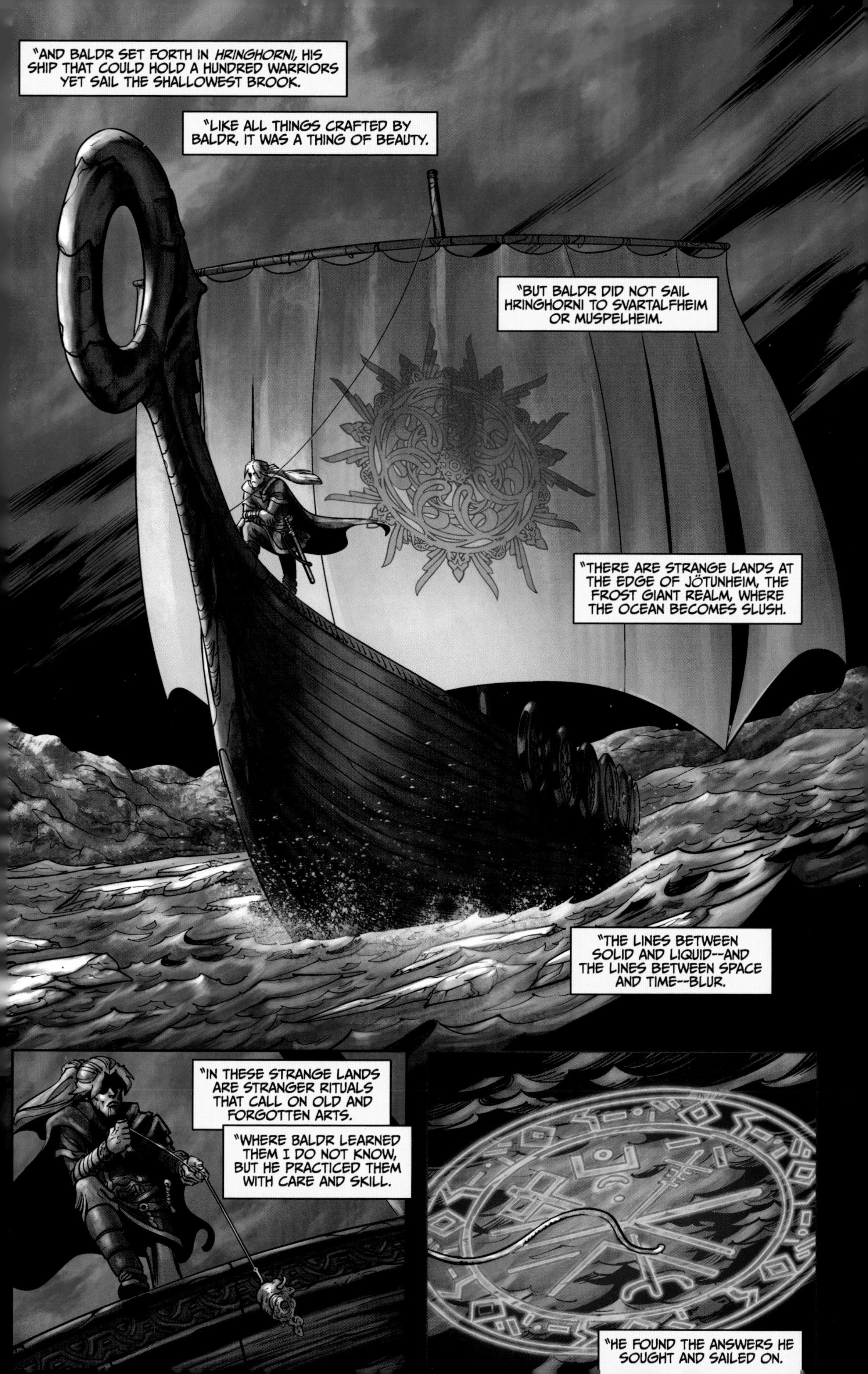
"AND BALDR SET FORTH IN *HRINGHORNI*, HIS SHIP THAT COULD HOLD A HUNDRED WARRIORS YET SAIL THE SHALLOWEST BROOK.
"LIKE ALL THINGS CRAFTED BY BALDR, IT WAS A THING OF BEAUTY.
"BUT BALDR DID NOT SAIL HRINGHORNI TO SVARTALFHEIM OR MUSPELHEIM.
"THERE ARE STRANGE LANDS AT THE EDGE OF JÖTUNHEIM, THE FROST GIANT REALM, WHERE THE OCEAN BECOMES SLUSH.
"THE LINES BETWEEN SOLID AND LIQUID--AND THE LINES BETWEEN SPACE AND TIME--BLUR.
"IN THESE STRANGE LANDS ARE STRANGER RITUALS THAT CALL ON OLD AND FORGOTTEN ARTS.
"WHERE BALDR LEARNED THEM I DO NOT KNOW, BUT HE PRACTICED THEM WITH CARE AND SKILL.
"HE FOUND THE ANSWERS HE SOUGHT AND SAILED ON.

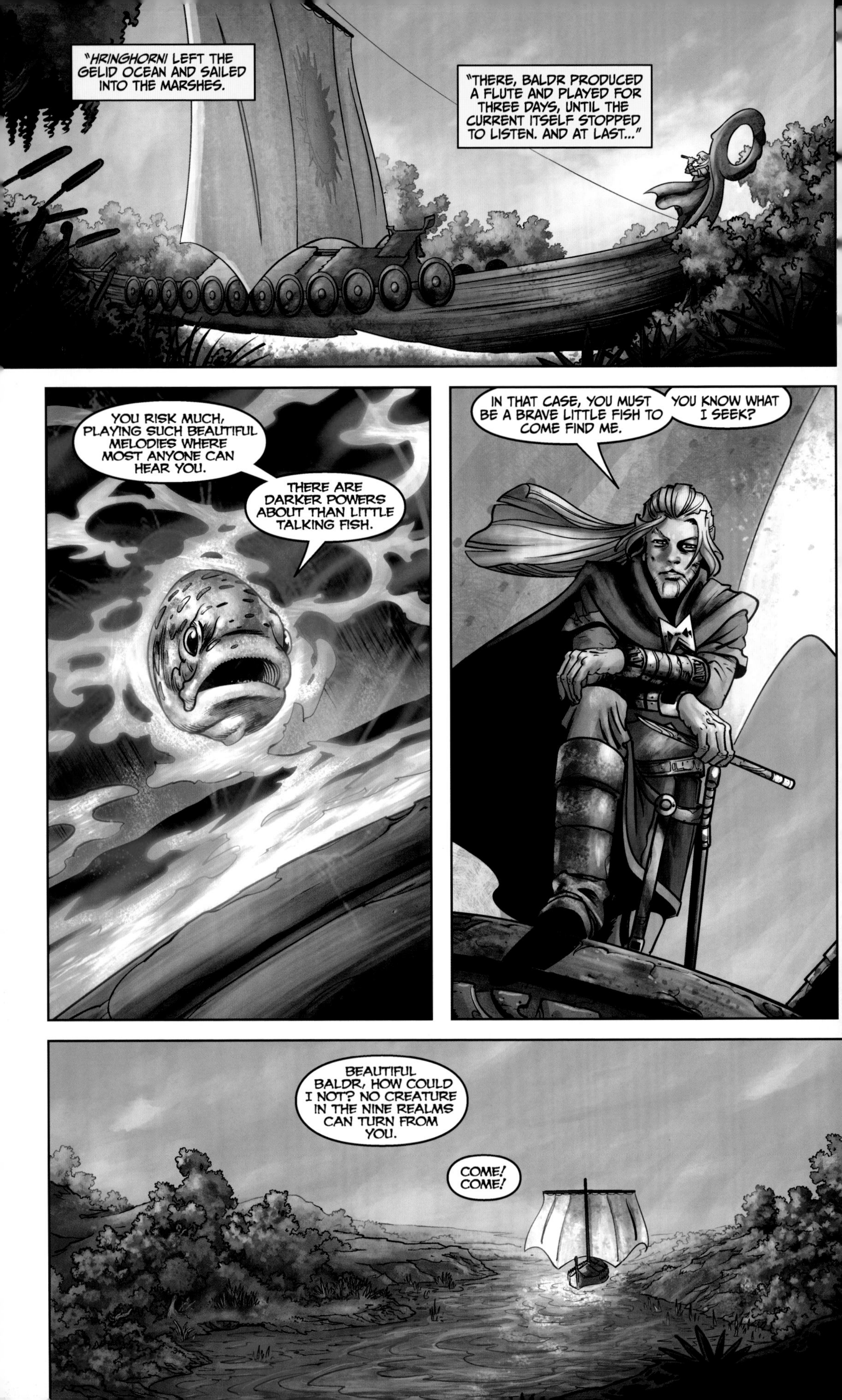
"HRINGHORNI LEFT THE GELID OCEAN AND SAILED INTO THE MARSHES.
"THERE, BALDR PRODUCED A FLUTE AND PLAYED FOR THREE DAYS, UNTIL THE CURRENT ITSELF STOPPED TO LISTEN. AND AT LAST..."
YOU RISK MUCH, PLAYING SUCH BEAUTIFUL MELODIES WHERE MOST ANYONE CAN HEAR YOU.
THERE ARE DARKER POWERS ABOUT THAN LITTLE TALKING FISH.
IN THAT CASE, YOU MUST BE A BRAVE LITTLE FISH TO COME FIND ME.
YOU KNOW WHAT I SEEK?
BEAUTIFUL BALDR, HOW COULD I NOT? NO CREATURE IN THE NINE REALMS CAN TURN FROM YOU.
COME! COME!

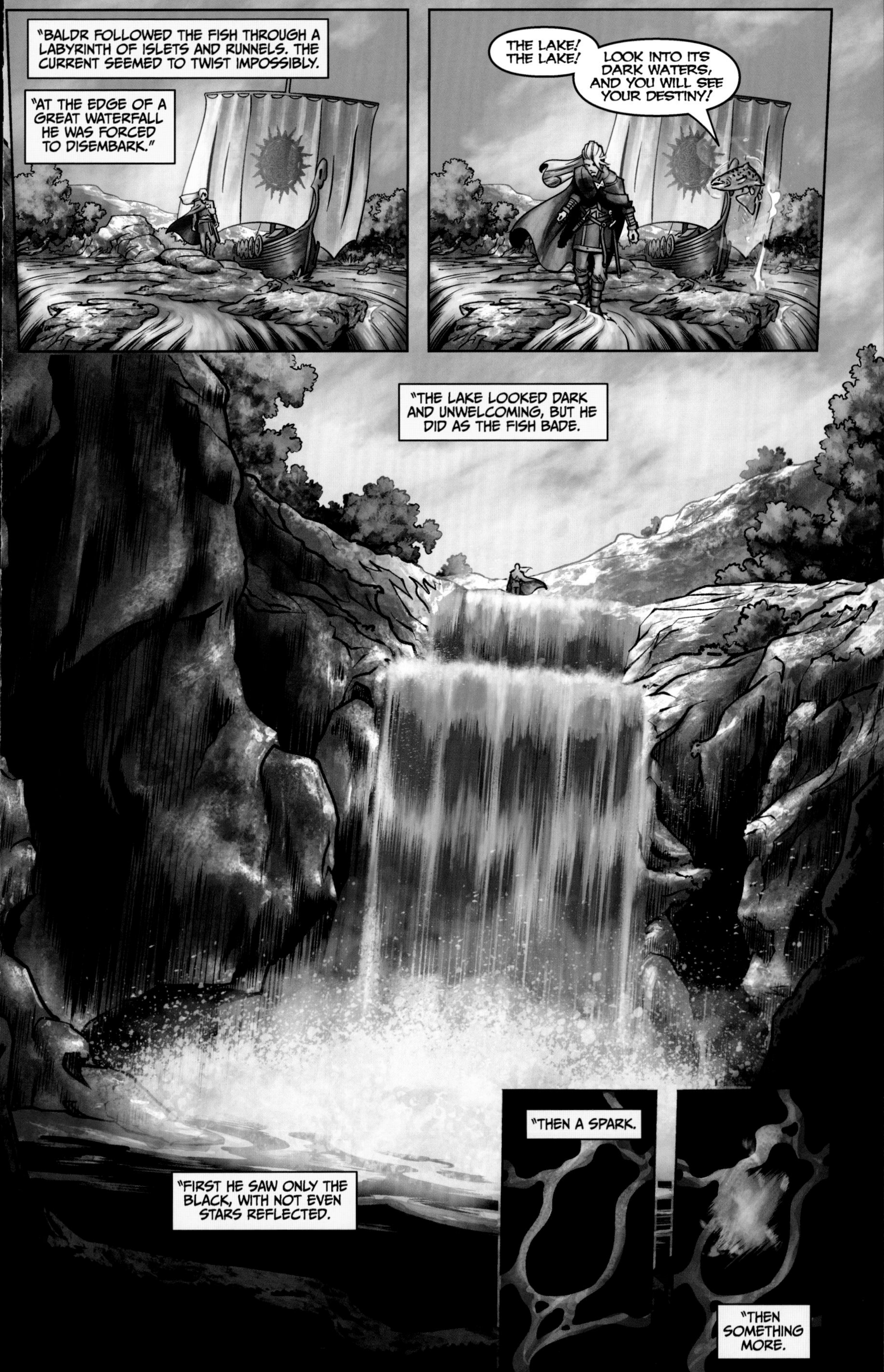
"BALDR FOLLOWED THE FISH THROUGH A LABYRINTH OF ISLETS AND RUNNELS. THE CURRENT SEEMED TO TWIST IMPOSSIBLY.
"AT THE EDGE OF A GREAT WATERFALL HE WAS FORCED TO DISEMBARK."
THE LAKE! THE LAKE!
LOOK INTO ITS DARK WATERS, AND YOU WILL SEE YOUR DESTINY!
"THE LAKE LOOKED DARK AND UNWELCOMING, BUT HE DID AS THE FISH BADE.
"FIRST HE SAW ONLY THE BLACK, WITH NOT EVEN STARS REFLECTED.
"THEN A SPARK.
"THEN SOMETHING MORE.

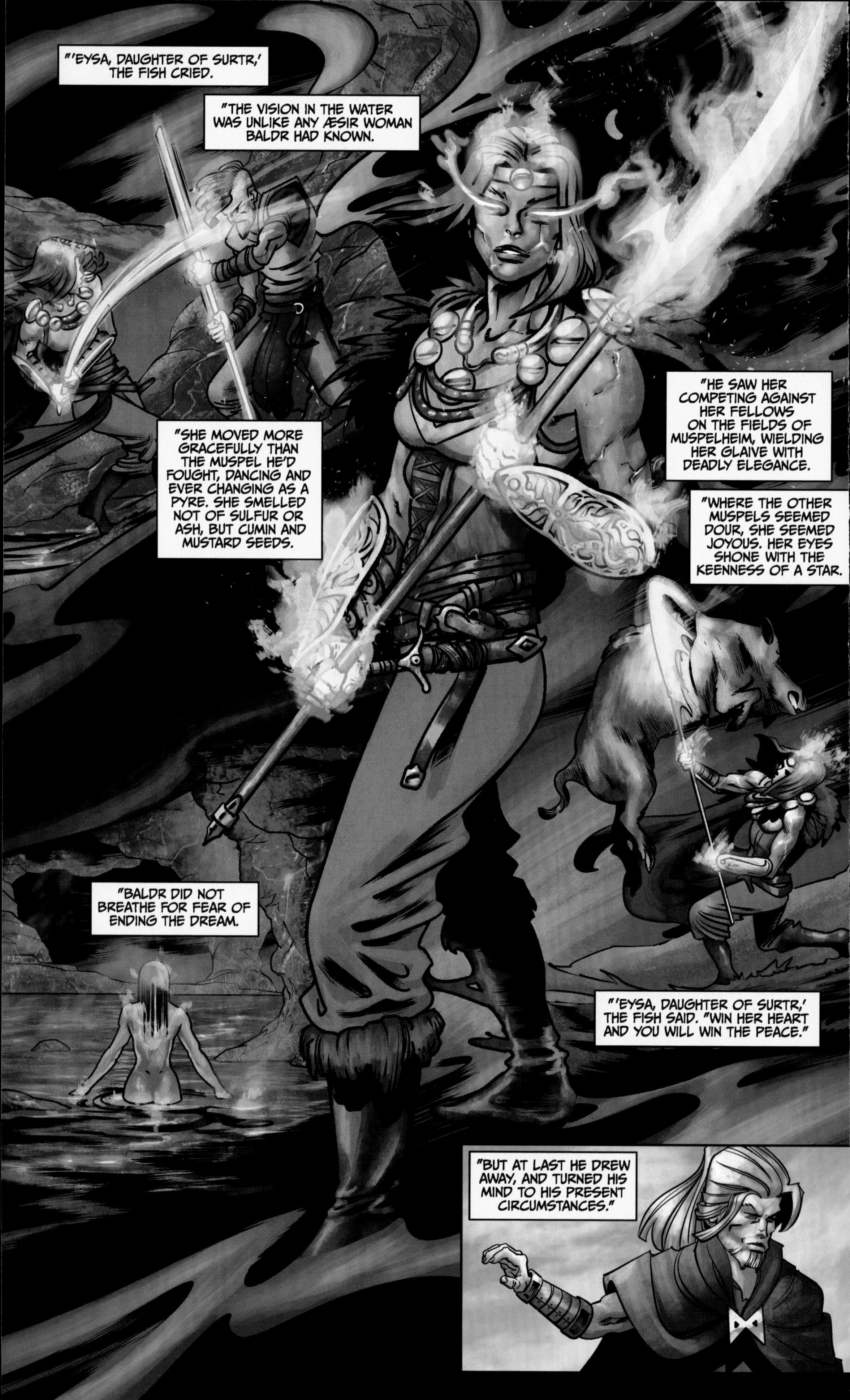
"'EYSA, DAUGHTER OF SURTR,' THE FISH CRIED.
"THE VISION IN THE WATER WAS UNLIKE ANY ÆSIR WOMAN BALDR HAD KNOWN.
"SHE MOVED MORE GRACEFULLY THAN THE MUSPEL HE'D FOUGHT, DANCING AND EVER CHANGING AS A PYRE. SHE SMELLED NOT OF SULFUR OR ASH, BUT CUMIN AND MUSTARD SEEDS.
"HE SAW HER COMPETING AGAINST HER FELLOWS ON THE FIELDS OF MUSPELHEIM, WIELDING HER GLAIVE WITH DEADLY ELEGANCE.
"WHERE THE OTHER MUSPELS SEEMED DOUR, SHE SEEMED JOYOUS. HER EYES SHONE WITH THE KEENNESS OF A STAR.
"BALDR DID NOT BREATHE FOR FEAR OF ENDING THE DREAM.
"'EYSA, DAUGHTER OF SURTR,' THE FISH SAID. "WIN HER HEART AND YOU WILL WIN THE PEACE."
"BUT AT LAST HE DREW AWAY, AND TURNED HIS MIND TO HIS PRESENT CIRCUMSTANCES."

WILL YOU HELP ME?

OH! YOU FLATTER A LITTLE TALKING FISH, BUT I HAVE DONE ALL I CAN.

AND WHAT OF LOKI? HAS HE DONE ALL HE CAN?

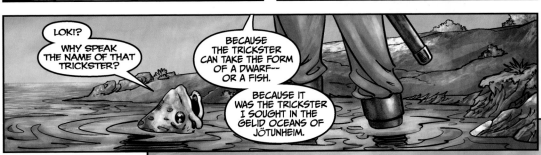

LOKI!? WHY SPEAK THE NAME OF THAT TRICKSTER?

BECAUSE THE TRICKSTER CAN TAKE THE FORM OF A DWARF-- OR A FISH.

BECAUSE IT WAS THE TRICKSTER I SOUGHT IN THE GELID OCEANS OF JÖTUNHEIM.

IF I AM TO FORGE PEACE BETWEEN SVARTALFHEIM AND MUSPELHEIM I WILL NEED A MENTOR IN THE ART OF DIPLOMACY--AND NONE IS SHREWDER THAN LOKI.

ALREADY YOU'VE SHOWN ME EYSA, BUT TO SEE A MAP IS NOT TO WALK A ROAD.

YOUR FATHER WOULD STRIKE ME DOWN ON THE SPOT.

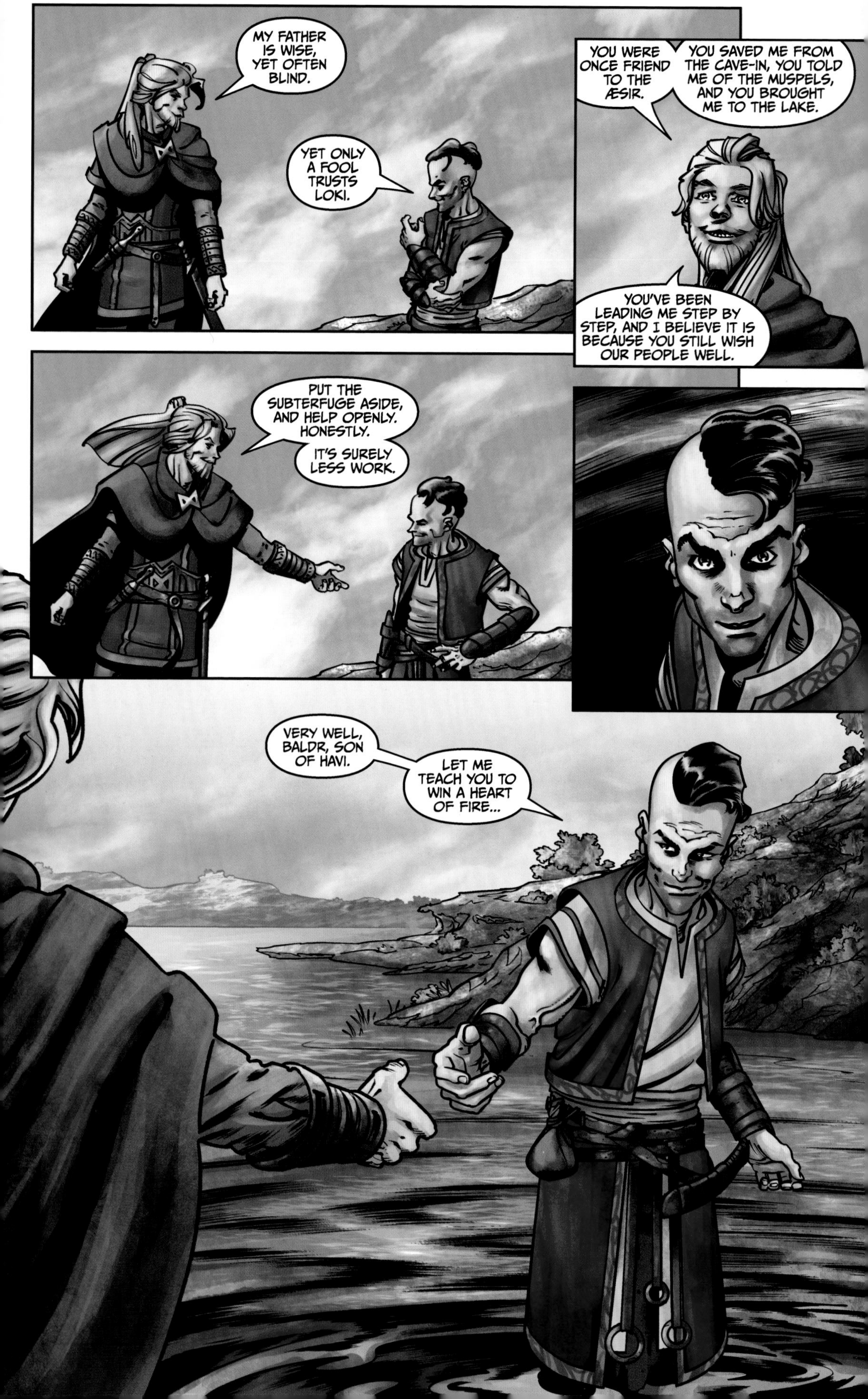
MY FATHER IS WISE, YET OFTEN BLIND.
YET ONLY A FOOL TRUSTS LOKI.
YOU WERE ONCE FRIEND TO THE ÆSIR.
YOU SAVED ME FROM THE CAVE-IN, YOU TOLD ME OF THE MUSPELS, AND YOU BROUGHT ME TO THE LAKE.
YOU'VE BEEN LEADING ME STEP BY STEP, AND I BELIEVE IT IS BECAUSE YOU STILL WISH OUR PEOPLE WELL.
PUT THE SUBTERFUGE ASIDE, AND HELP OPENLY. HONESTLY.
IT'S SURELY LESS WORK.
VERY WELL, BALDR, SON OF HAVI.
LET ME TEACH YOU TO WIN A HEART OF FIRE...

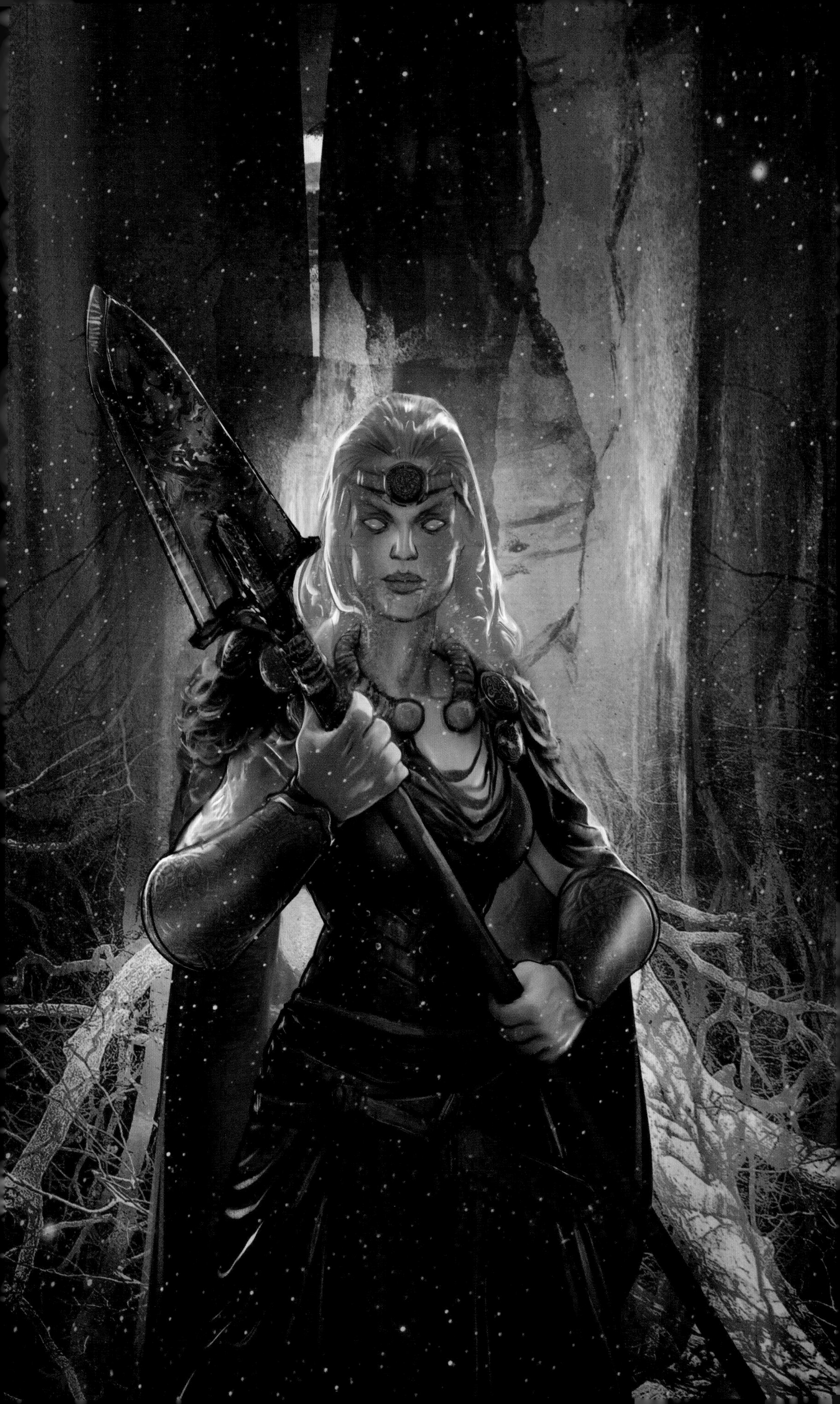

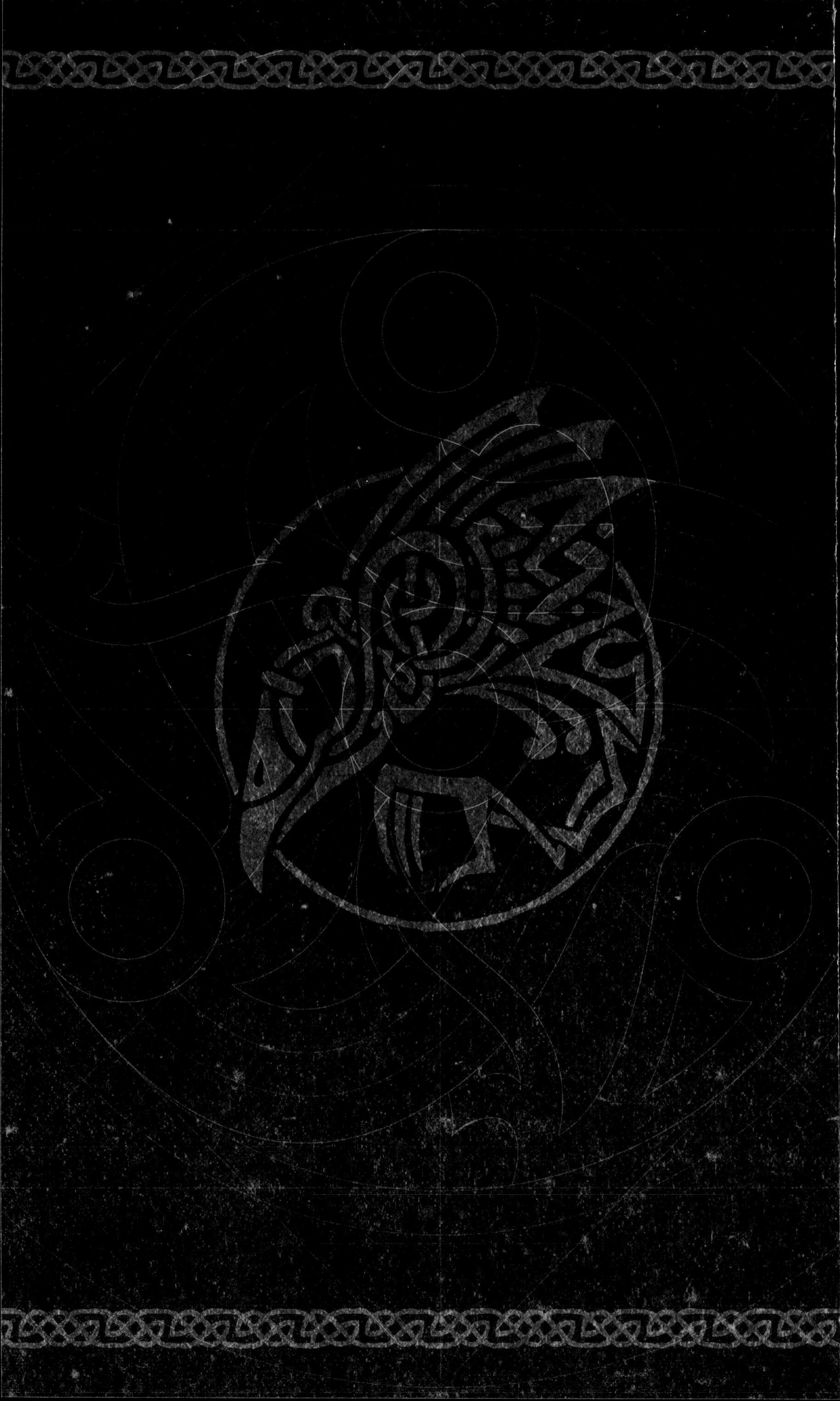

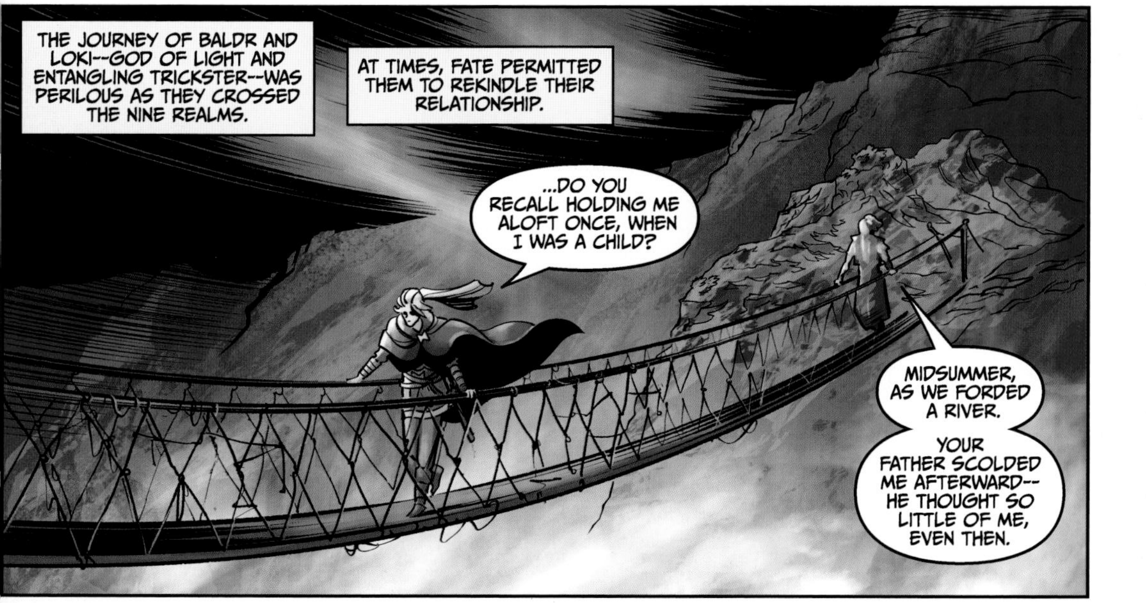
THE JOURNEY OF BALDR AND LOKI--GOD OF LIGHT AND ENTANGLING TRICKSTER--WAS PERILOUS AS THEY CROSSED THE NINE REALMS.
AT TIMES, FATE PERMITTED THEM TO REKINDLE THEIR RELATIONSHIP.
...DO YOU RECALL HOLDING ME ALOFT ONCE, WHEN I WAS A CHILD?
MIDSUMMER, AS WE FORDED A RIVER.
YOUR FATHER SCOLDED ME AFTERWARD--HE THOUGHT SO LITTLE OF ME, EVEN THEN.

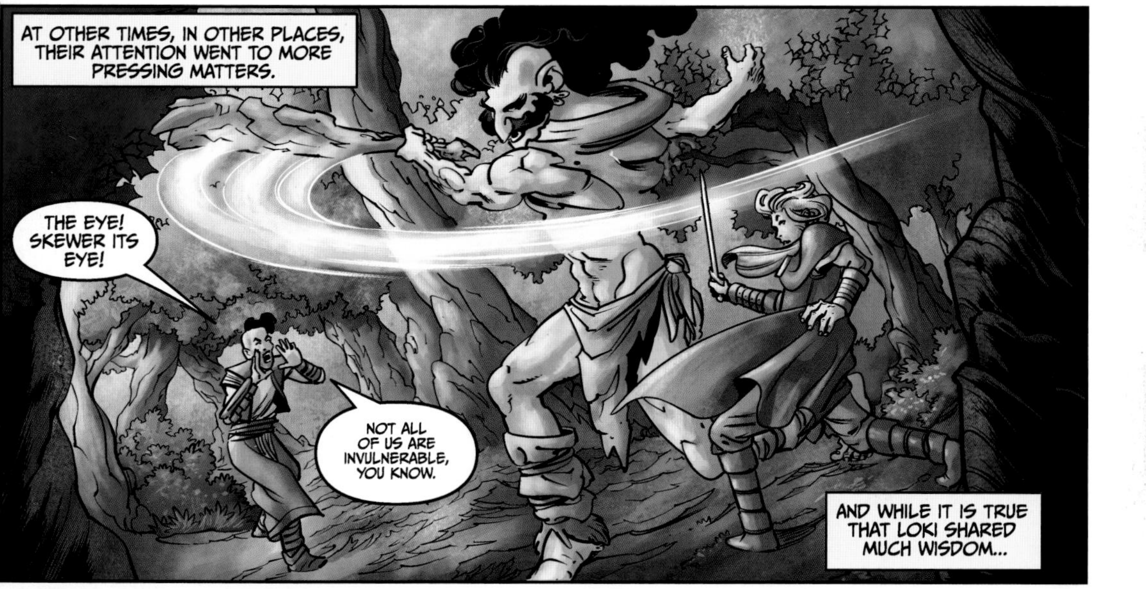
AT OTHER TIMES, IN OTHER PLACES, THEIR ATTENTION WENT TO MORE PRESSING MATTERS.
THE EYE! SKEWER ITS EYE!
NOT ALL OF US ARE INVULNERABLE, YOU KNOW.
AND WHILE IT IS TRUE THAT LOKI SHARED MUCH WISDOM...

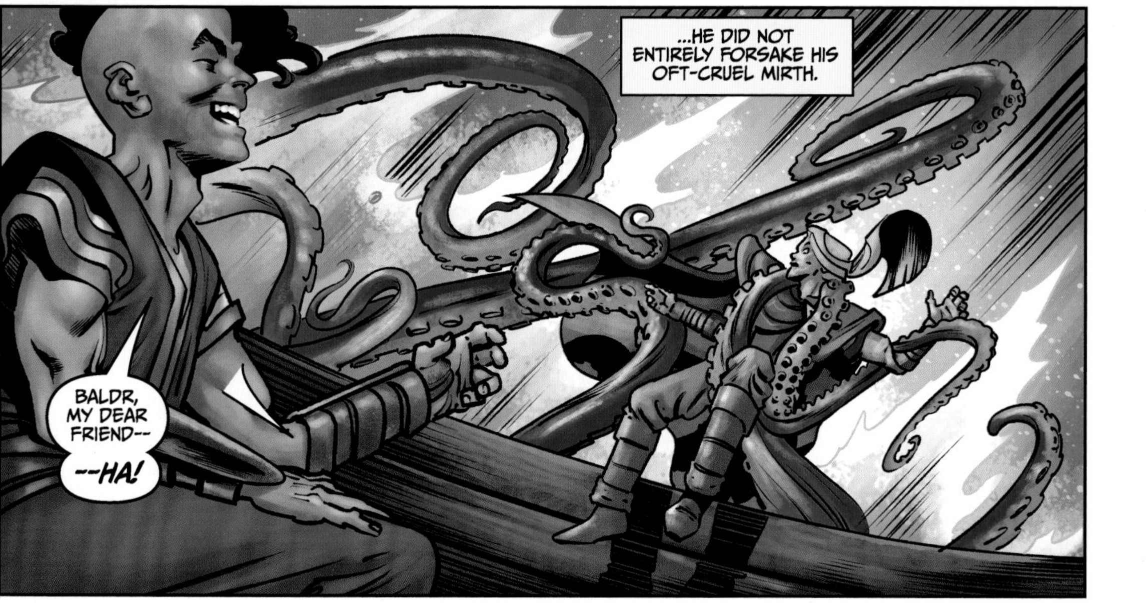
...HE DID NOT ENTIRELY FORSAKE HIS OFT-CRUEL MIRTH.
BALDR, MY DEAR FRIEND--
--HA!

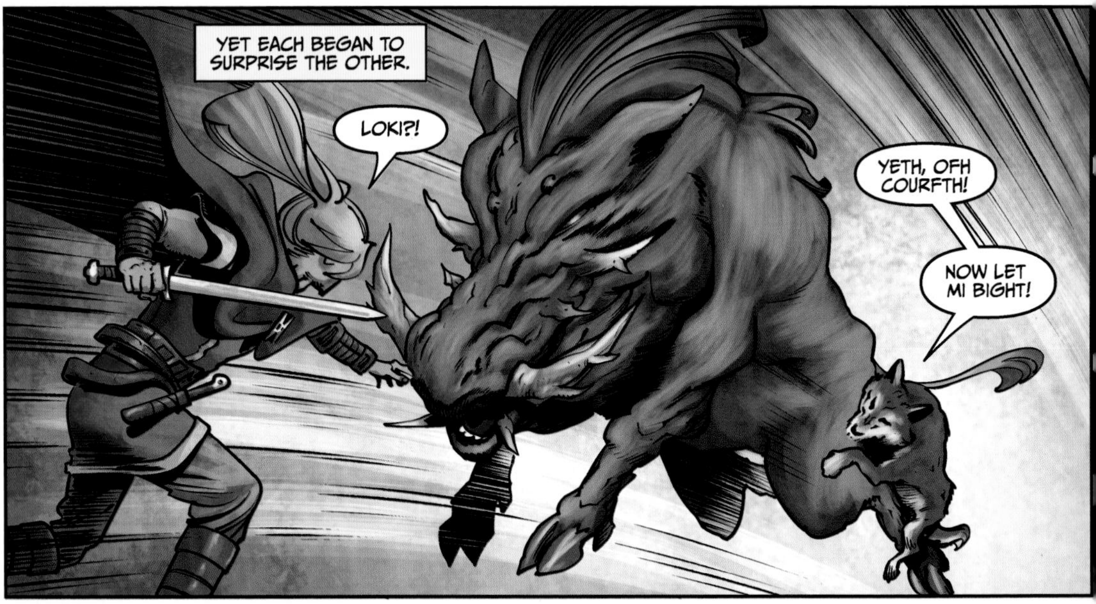
YET EACH BEGAN TO SURPRISE THE OTHER.
LOKI?!
YETH, OFH COURFTH!
NOW LET MI BIGHT!

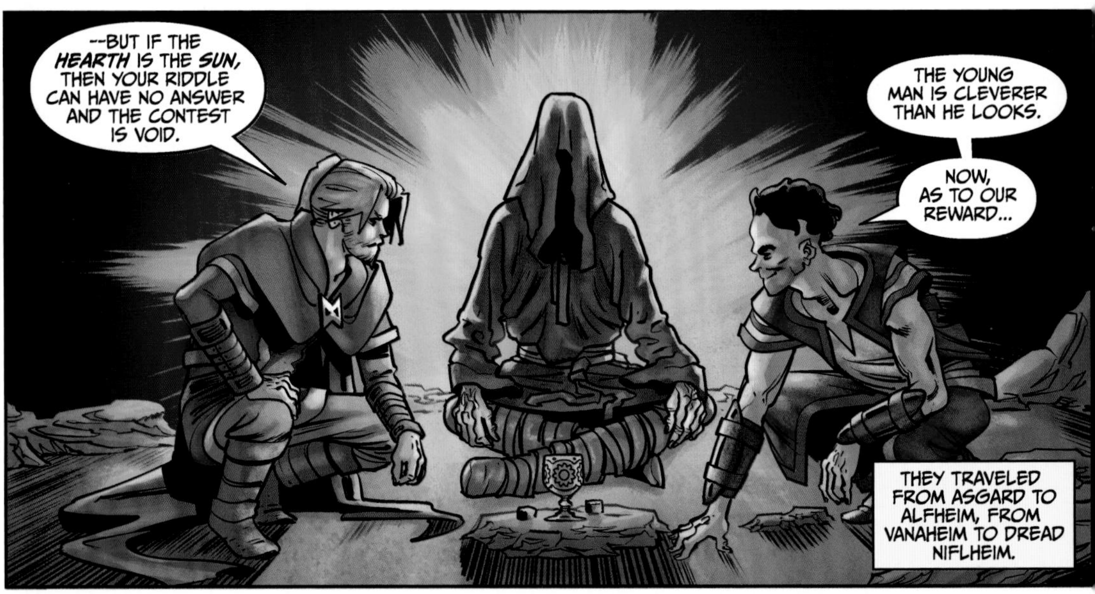
--BUT IF THE *HEARTH* IS THE *SUN,* THEN YOUR RIDDLE CAN HAVE NO ANSWER AND THE CONTEST IS VOID.
THE YOUNG MAN IS CLEVERER THAN HE LOOKS.
NOW, AS TO OUR REWARD...
THEY TRAVELED FROM ASGARD TO ALFHEIM, FROM VANAHEIM TO DREAD NIFLHEIM.

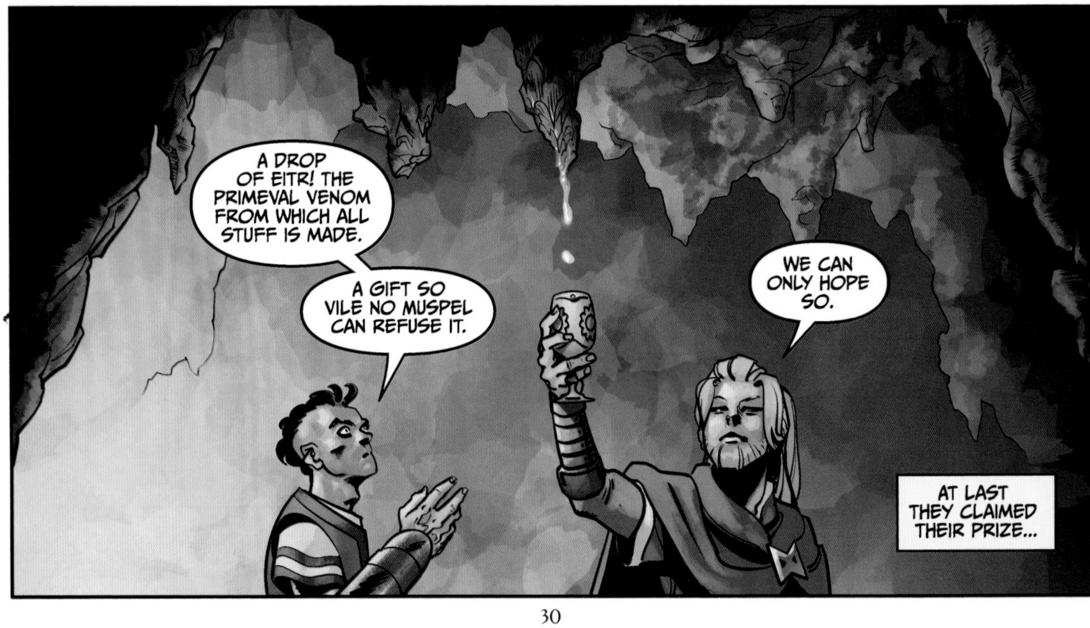
A DROP OF EITR! THE PRIMEVAL VENOM FROM WHICH ALL STUFF IS MADE.
A GIFT SO VILE NO MUSPEL CAN REFUSE IT.
WE CAN ONLY HOPE SO.
AT LAST THEY CLAIMED THEIR PRIZE...

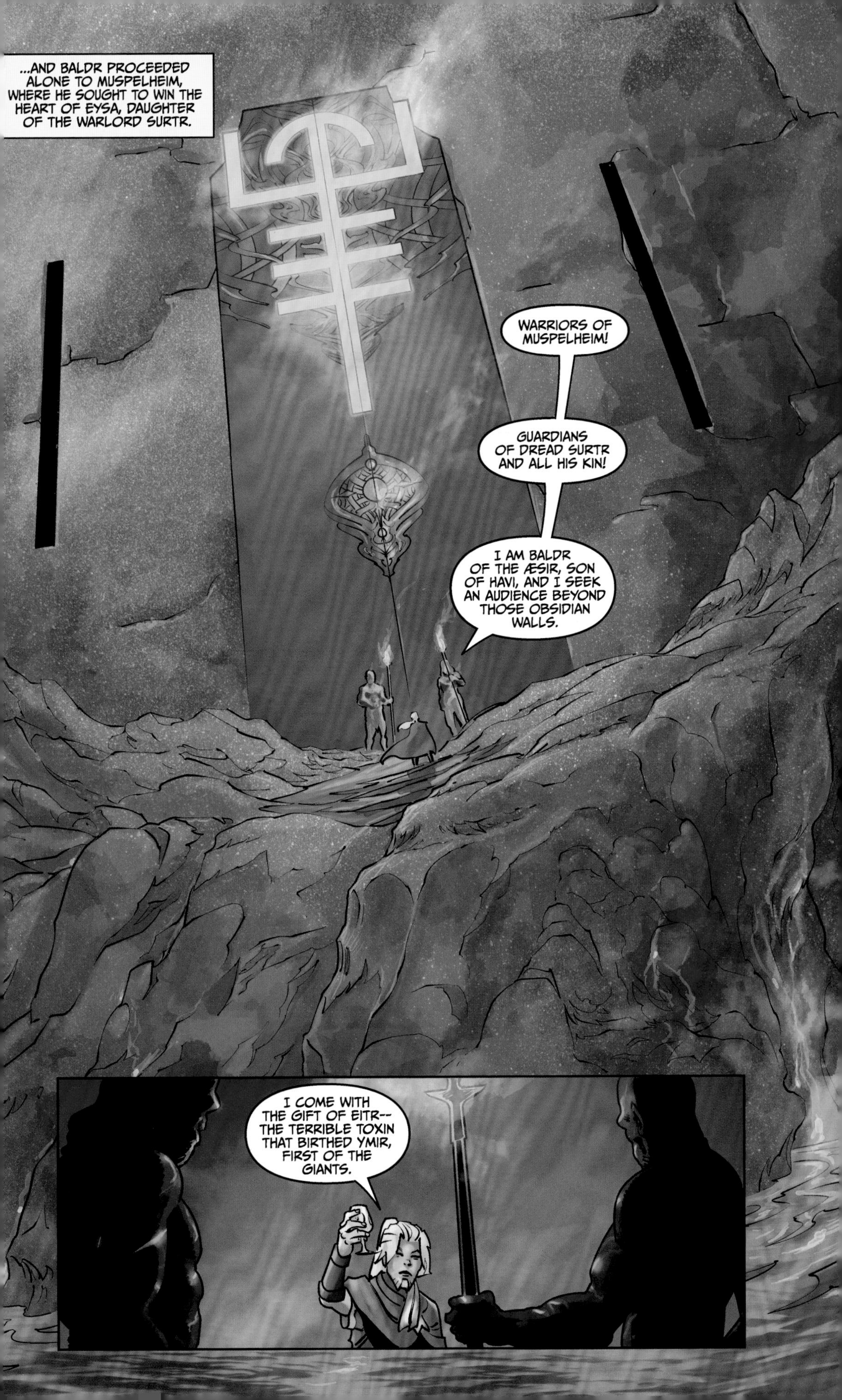
...AND BALDR PROCEEDED ALONE TO MUSPELHEIM, WHERE HE SOUGHT TO WIN THE HEART OF EYSA, DAUGHTER OF THE WARLORD SURTR.
WARRIORS OF MUSPELHEIM!
GUARDIANS OF DREAD SURTR AND ALL HIS KIN!
I AM BALDR OF THE ÆSIR, SON OF HAVI, AND I SEEK AN AUDIENCE BEYOND THOSE OBSIDIAN WALLS.
I COME WITH THE GIFT OF EITR-- THE TERRIBLE TOXIN THAT BIRTHED YMIR, FIRST OF THE GIANTS.

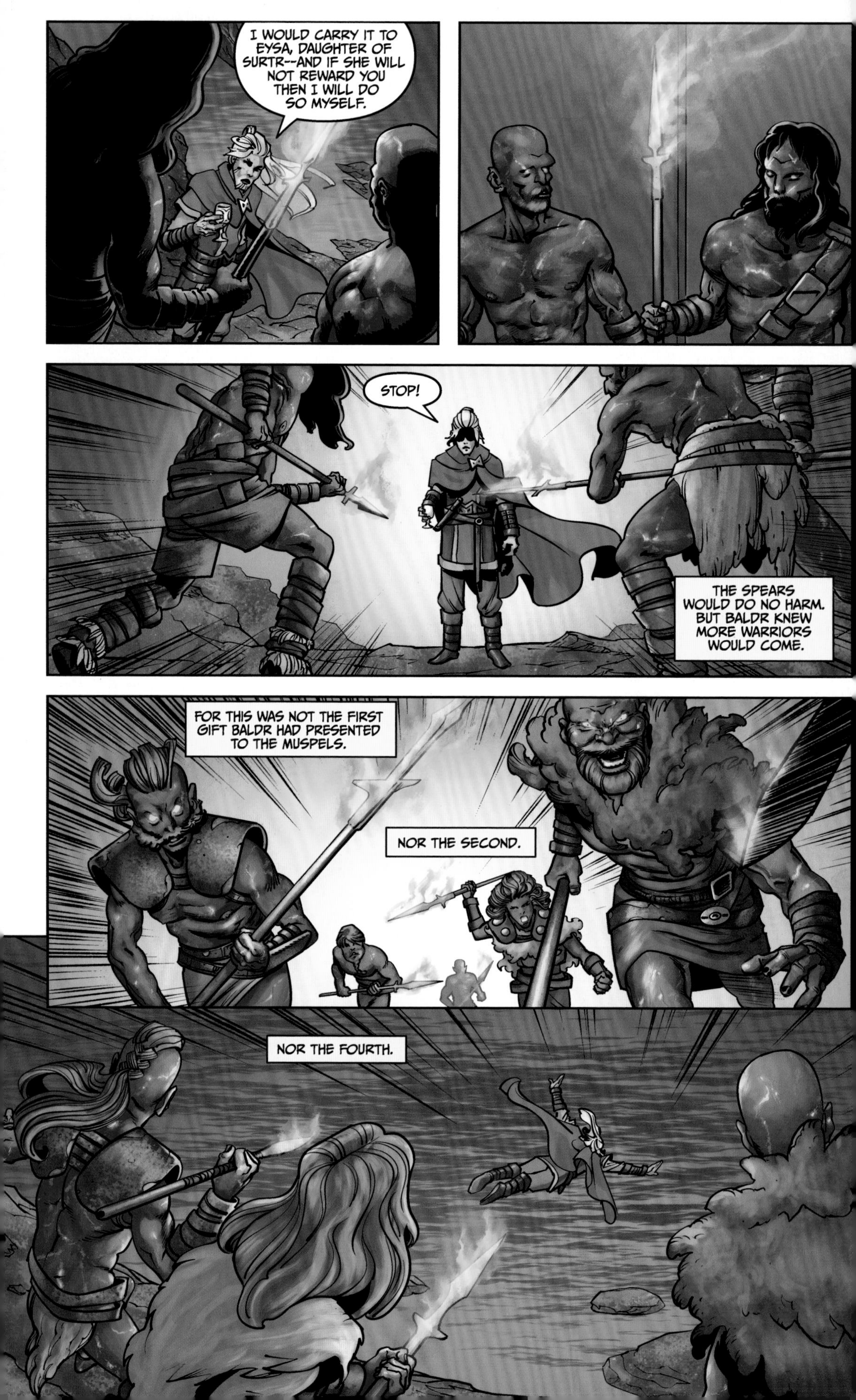

I WOULD CARRY IT TO EYSA, DAUGHTER OF SURTR--AND IF SHE WILL NOT REWARD YOU THEN I WILL DO SO MYSELF.
STOP!
THE SPEARS WOULD DO NO HARM. BUT BALDR KNEW MORE WARRIORS WOULD COME.
FOR THIS WAS NOT THE FIRST GIFT BALDR HAD PRESENTED TO THE MUSPELS.
NOR THE SECOND.
NOR THE FOURTH.

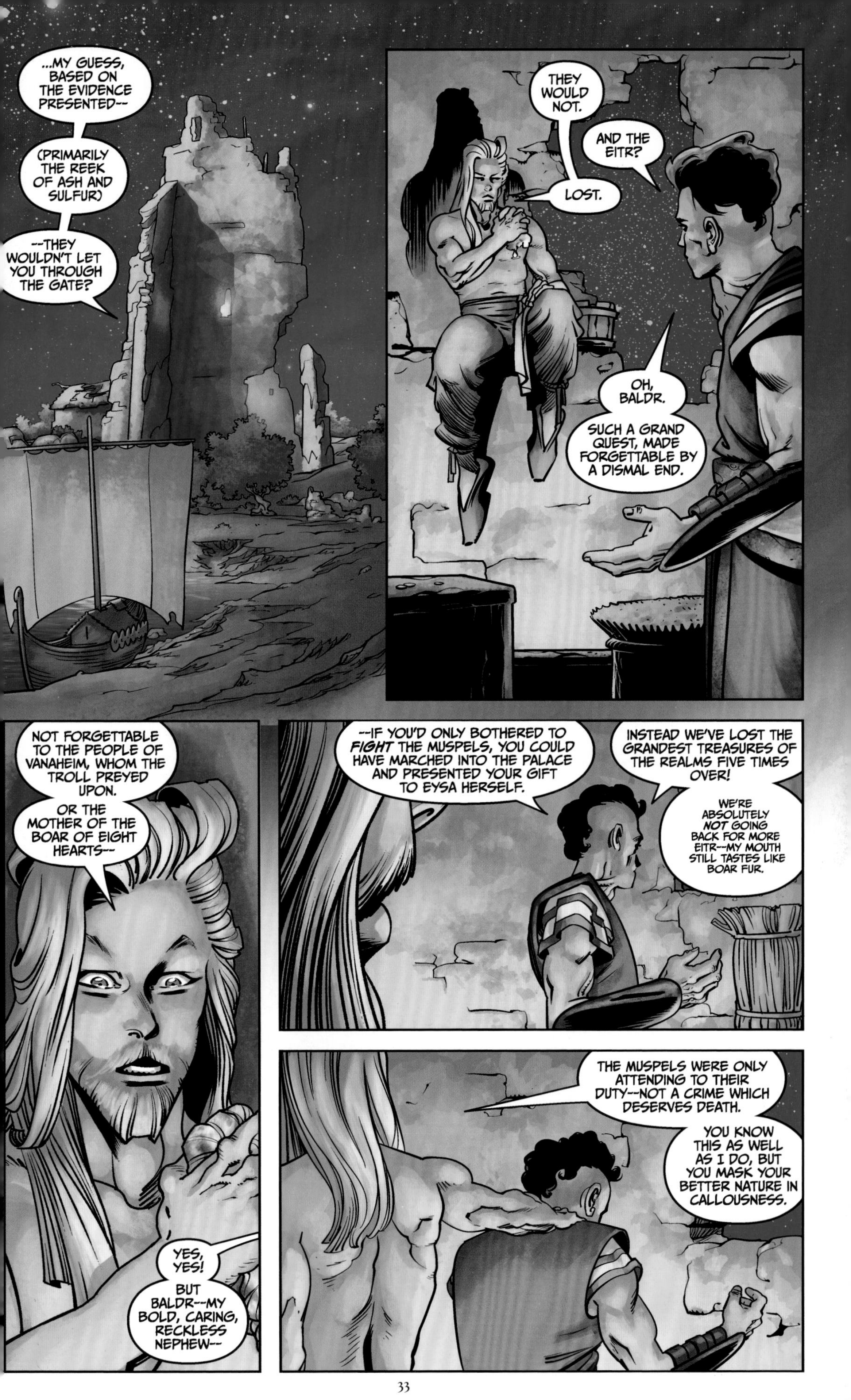
...MY GUESS, BASED ON THE EVIDENCE PRESENTED--
(PRIMARILY THE REEK OF ASH AND SULFUR)
--THEY WOULDN'T LET YOU THROUGH THE GATE?
THEY WOULD NOT.
AND THE EITR?
LOST.
OH, BALDR.
SUCH A GRAND QUEST, MADE FORGETTABLE BY A DISMAL END.
NOT FORGETTABLE TO THE PEOPLE OF VANAHEIM, WHOM THE TROLL PREYED UPON.
OR THE MOTHER OF THE BOAR OF EIGHT HEARTS--
YES, YES!
BUT BALDR--MY BOLD, CARING, RECKLESS NEPHEW--
--IF YOU'D ONLY BOTHERED TO *FIGHT* THE MUSPELS, YOU COULD HAVE MARCHED INTO THE PALACE AND PRESENTED YOUR GIFT TO EYSA HERSELF.
INSTEAD WE'VE LOST THE GRANDEST TREASURES OF THE REALMS FIVE TIMES OVER!
WE'RE ABSOLUTELY *NOT* GOING BACK FOR MORE EITR--MY MOUTH STILL TASTES LIKE BOAR FUR.
THE MUSPELS WERE ONLY ATTENDING TO THEIR DUTY--NOT A CRIME WHICH DESERVES DEATH.
YOU KNOW THIS AS WELL AS I DO, BUT YOU MASK YOUR BETTER NATURE IN CALLOUSNESS.

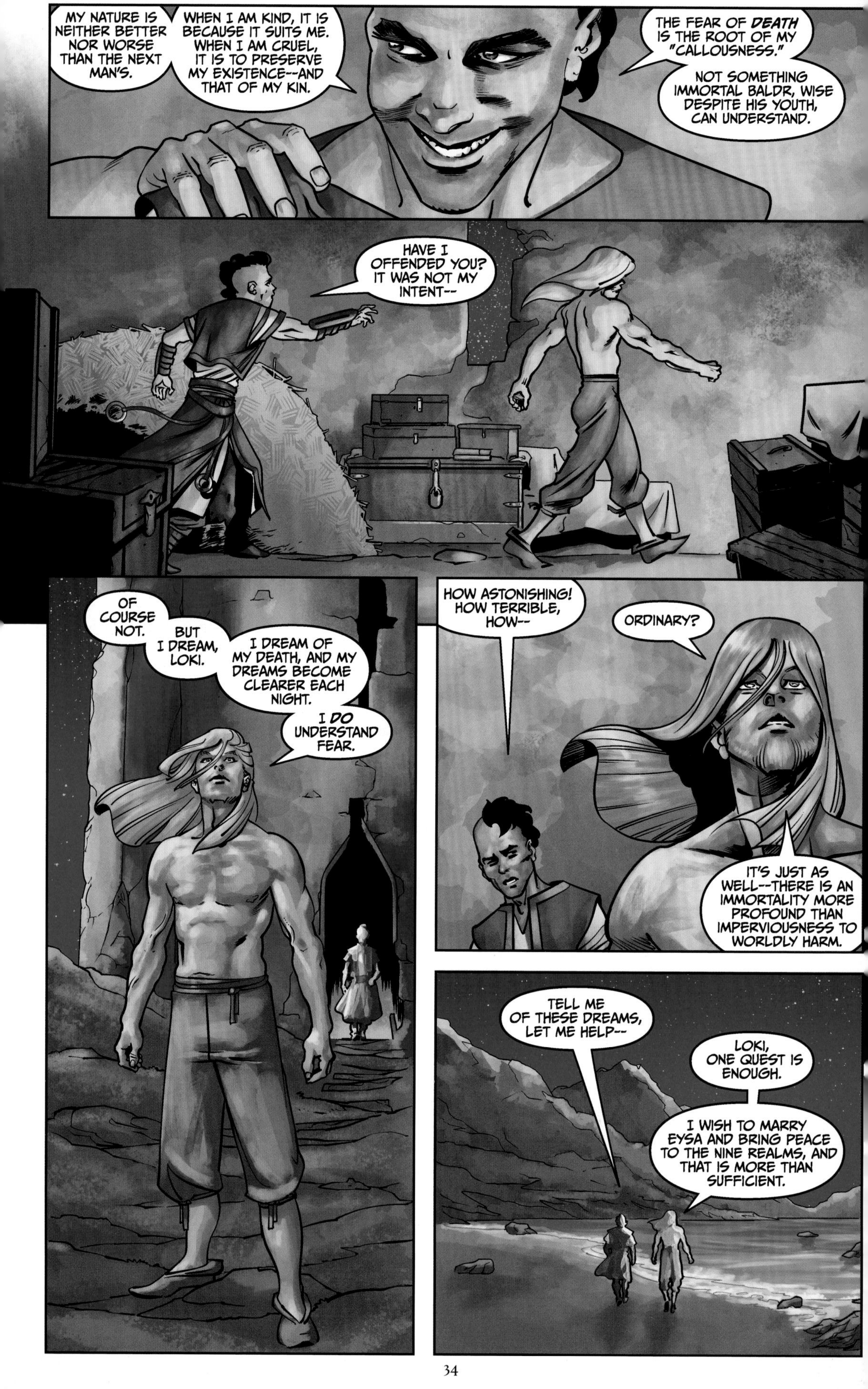
MY NATURE IS NEITHER BETTER NOR WORSE THAN THE NEXT MAN'S.
WHEN I AM KIND, IT IS BECAUSE IT SUITS ME. WHEN I AM CRUEL, IT IS TO PRESERVE MY EXISTENCE--AND THAT OF MY KIN.
THE FEAR OF *DEATH* IS THE ROOT OF MY "CALLOUSNESS."
NOT SOMETHING IMMORTAL BALDR, WISE DESPITE HIS YOUTH, CAN UNDERSTAND.
HAVE I OFFENDED YOU? IT WAS NOT MY INTENT--
OF COURSE NOT.
BUT I DREAM, LOKI.
I DREAM OF MY DEATH, AND MY DREAMS BECOME CLEARER EACH NIGHT.
I *DO* UNDERSTAND FEAR.
HOW ASTONISHING! HOW TERRIBLE, HOW--
ORDINARY?
IT'S JUST AS WELL--THERE IS AN IMMORTALITY MORE PROFOUND THAN IMPERVIOUSNESS TO WORLDLY HARM.
TELL ME OF THESE DREAMS, LET ME HELP--
LOKI, ONE QUEST IS ENOUGH.
I WISH TO MARRY EYSA AND BRING PEACE TO THE NINE REALMS, AND THAT IS MORE THAN SUFFICIENT.

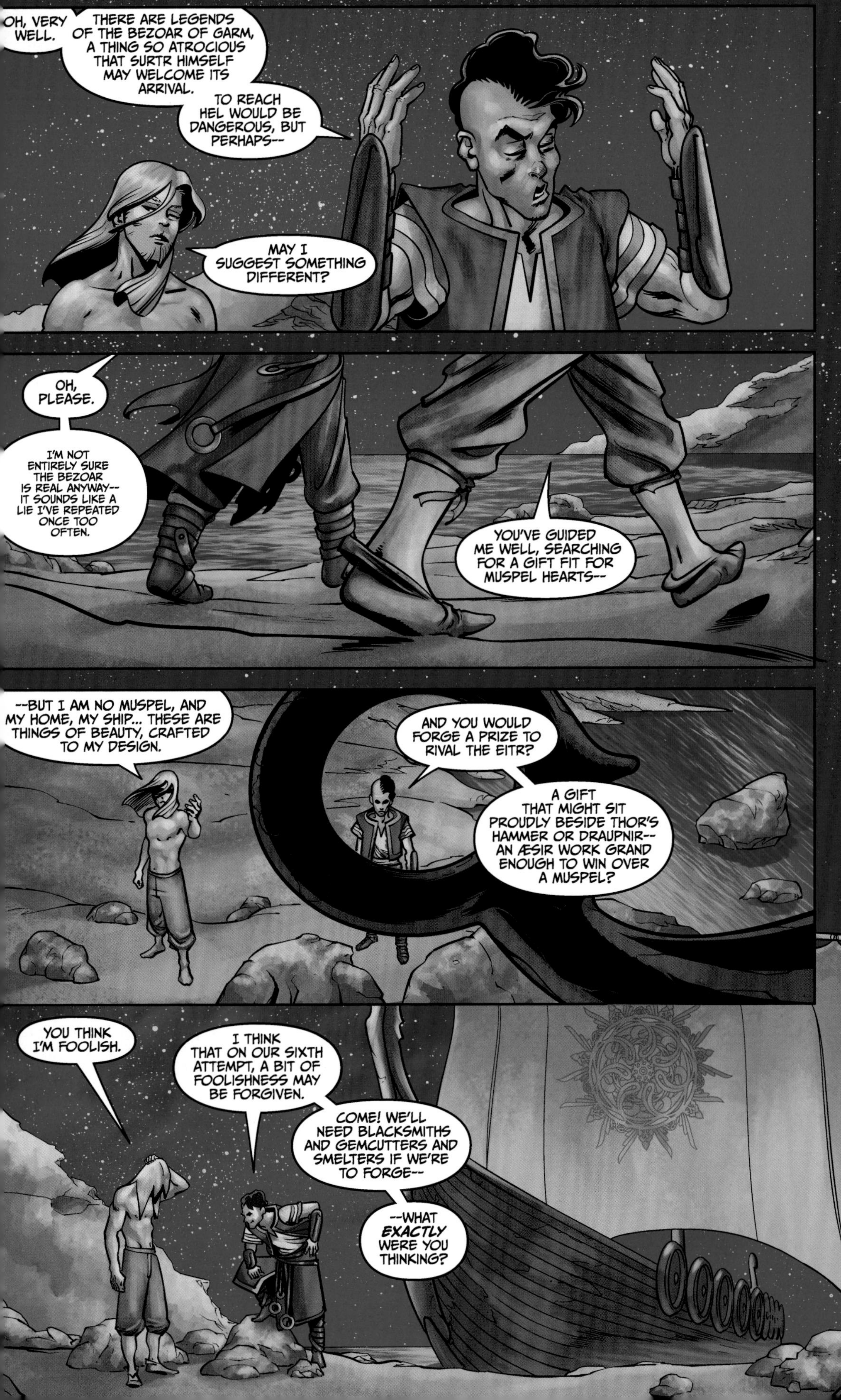

OH, VERY WELL.
THERE ARE LEGENDS OF THE BEZOAR OF GARM, A THING SO ATROCIOUS THAT SURTR HIMSELF MAY WELCOME ITS ARRIVAL.
TO REACH HEL WOULD BE DANGEROUS, BUT PERHAPS--
MAY I SUGGEST SOMETHING DIFFERENT?
OH, PLEASE.
I'M NOT ENTIRELY SURE THE BEZOAR IS REAL ANYWAY-- IT SOUNDS LIKE A LIE I'VE REPEATED ONCE TOO OFTEN.
YOU'VE GUIDED ME WELL, SEARCHING FOR A GIFT FIT FOR MUSPEL HEARTS--
--BUT I AM NO MUSPEL, AND MY HOME, MY SHIP... THESE ARE THINGS OF BEAUTY, CRAFTED TO MY DESIGN.
AND YOU WOULD FORGE A PRIZE TO RIVAL THE EITR?
A GIFT THAT MIGHT SIT PROUDLY BESIDE THOR'S HAMMER OR DRAUPNIR-- AN ÆSIR WORK GRAND ENOUGH TO WIN OVER A MUSPEL?
YOU THINK I'M FOOLISH.
I THINK THAT ON OUR SIXTH ATTEMPT, A BIT OF FOOLISHNESS MAY BE FORGIVEN.
COME! WE'LL NEED BLACKSMITHS AND GEMCUTTERS AND SMELTERS IF WE'RE TO FORGE--
--WHAT *EXACTLY* WERE YOU THINKING?

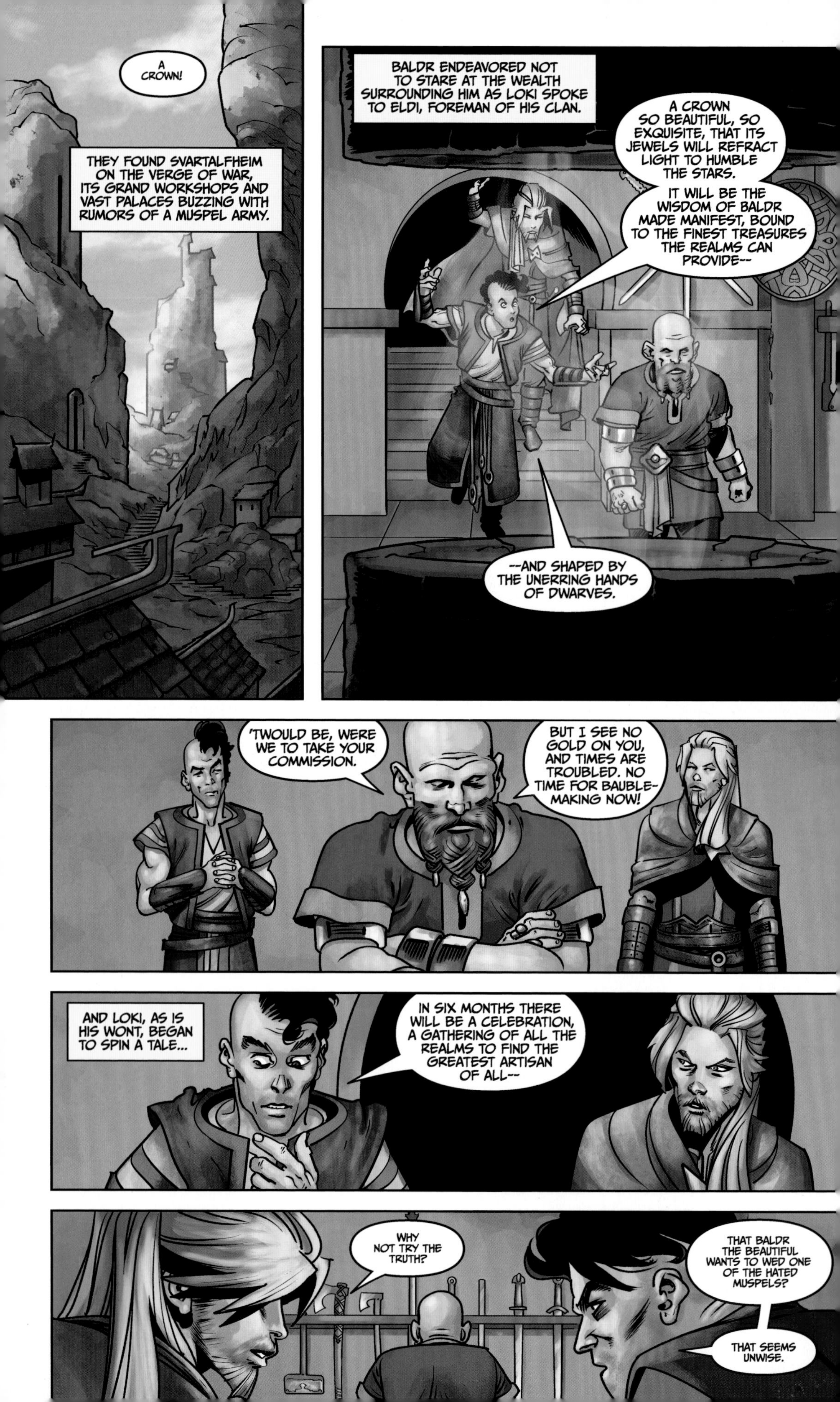
A CROWN!
THEY FOUND SVARTALFHEIM ON THE VERGE OF WAR, ITS GRAND WORKSHOPS AND VAST PALACES BUZZING WITH RUMORS OF A MUSPEL ARMY.
BALDR ENDEAVORED NOT TO STARE AT THE WEALTH SURROUNDING HIM AS LOKI SPOKE TO ELDI, FOREMAN OF HIS CLAN.
A CROWN SO BEAUTIFUL, SO EXQUISITE, THAT ITS JEWELS WILL REFRACT LIGHT TO HUMBLE THE STARS.
IT WILL BE THE WISDOM OF BALDR MADE MANIFEST, BOUND TO THE FINEST TREASURES THE REALMS CAN PROVIDE--
--AND SHAPED BY THE UNERRING HANDS OF DWARVES.
'TWOULD BE, WERE WE TO TAKE YOUR COMMISSION.
BUT I SEE NO GOLD ON YOU, AND TIMES ARE TROUBLED. NO TIME FOR BAUBLE-MAKING NOW!
AND LOKI, AS IS HIS WONT, BEGAN TO SPIN A TALE...
IN SIX MONTHS THERE WILL BE A CELEBRATION, A GATHERING OF ALL THE REALMS TO FIND THE GREATEST ARTISAN OF ALL--
WHY NOT TRY THE TRUTH?
THAT BALDR THE BEAUTIFUL WANTS TO WED ONE OF THE HATED MUSPELS?
THAT SEEMS UNWISE.

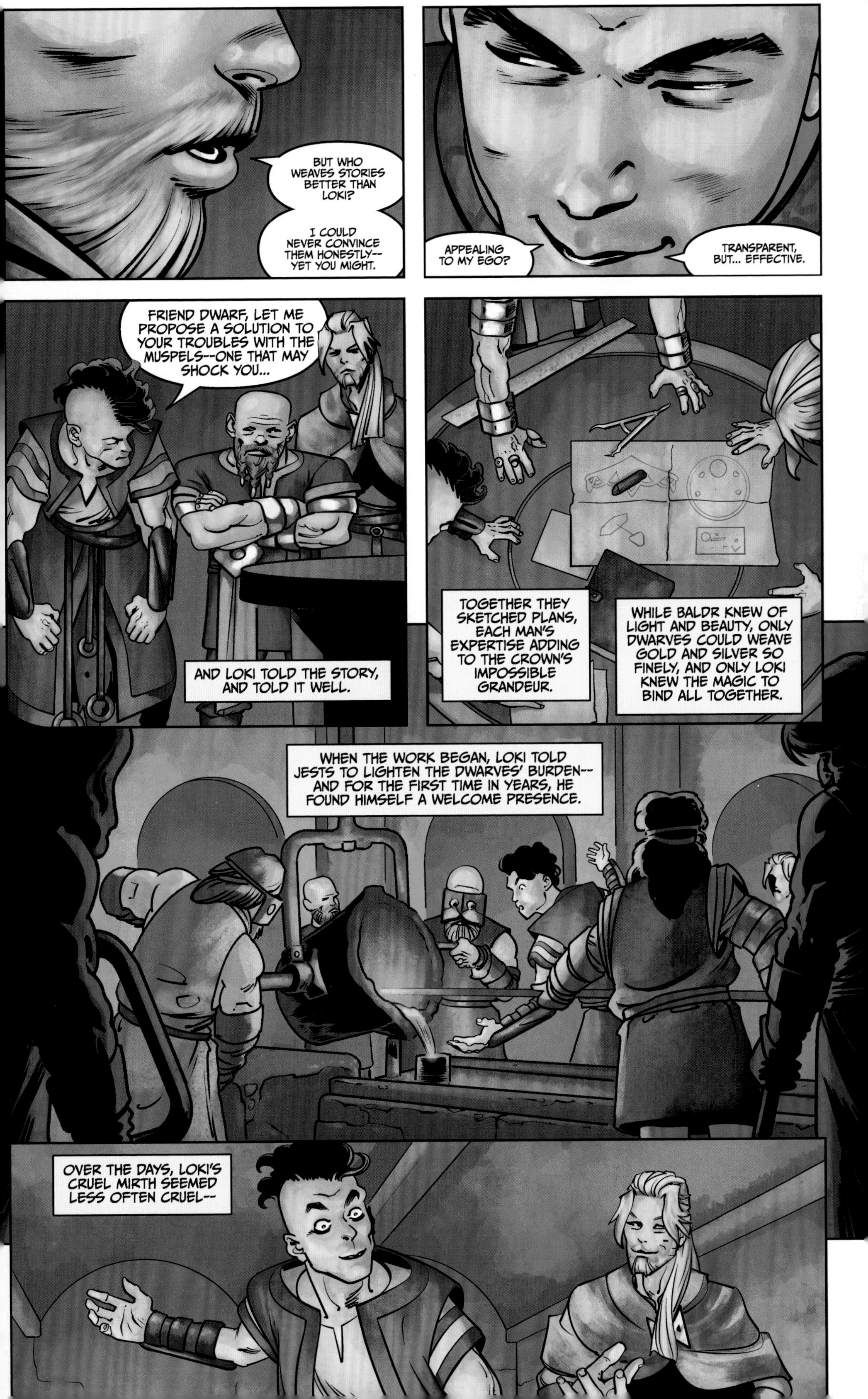
BUT WHO WEAVES STORIES BETTER THAN LOKI?
I COULD NEVER CONVINCE THEM HONESTLY-- YET YOU MIGHT.
APPEALING TO MY EGO?
TRANSPARENT, BUT... EFFECTIVE.
FRIEND DWARF, LET ME PROPOSE A SOLUTION TO YOUR TROUBLES WITH THE MUSPELS--ONE THAT MAY SHOCK YOU...
AND LOKI TOLD THE STORY, AND TOLD IT WELL.
TOGETHER THEY SKETCHED PLANS, EACH MAN'S EXPERTISE ADDING TO THE CROWN'S IMPOSSIBLE GRANDEUR.
WHILE BALDR KNEW OF LIGHT AND BEAUTY, ONLY DWARVES COULD WEAVE GOLD AND SILVER SO FINELY, AND ONLY LOKI KNEW THE MAGIC TO BIND ALL TOGETHER.
WHEN THE WORK BEGAN, LOKI TOLD JESTS TO LIGHTEN THE DWARVES' BURDEN-- AND FOR THE FIRST TIME IN YEARS, HE FOUND HIMSELF A WELCOME PRESENCE.
OVER THE DAYS, LOKI'S CRUEL MIRTH SEEMED LESS OFTEN CRUEL--

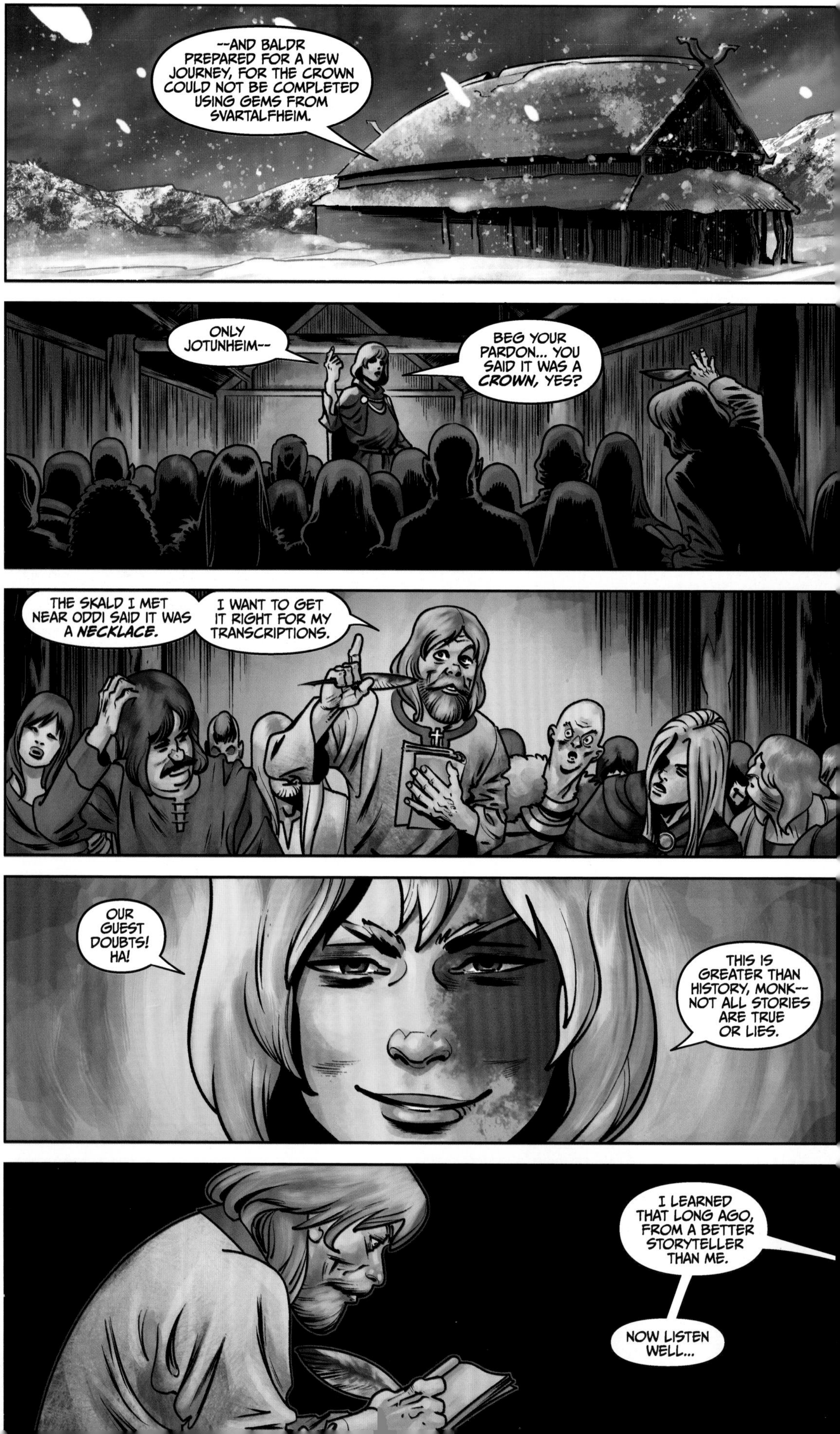
--AND BALDR PREPARED FOR A NEW JOURNEY, FOR THE CROWN COULD NOT BE COMPLETED USING GEMS FROM SVARTALFHEIM.
ONLY JOTUNHEIM--
BEG YOUR PARDON... YOU SAID IT WAS A *CROWN,* YES?
THE SKALD I MET NEAR ODDI SAID IT WAS A ***NECKLACE.***
I WANT TO GET IT RIGHT FOR MY TRANSCRIPTIONS.
OUR GUEST DOUBTS! HA!
THIS IS GREATER THAN HISTORY, MONK-- NOT ALL STORIES ARE TRUE OR LIES.
I LEARNED THAT LONG AGO, FROM A BETTER STORYTELLER THAN ME.
NOW LISTEN WELL...

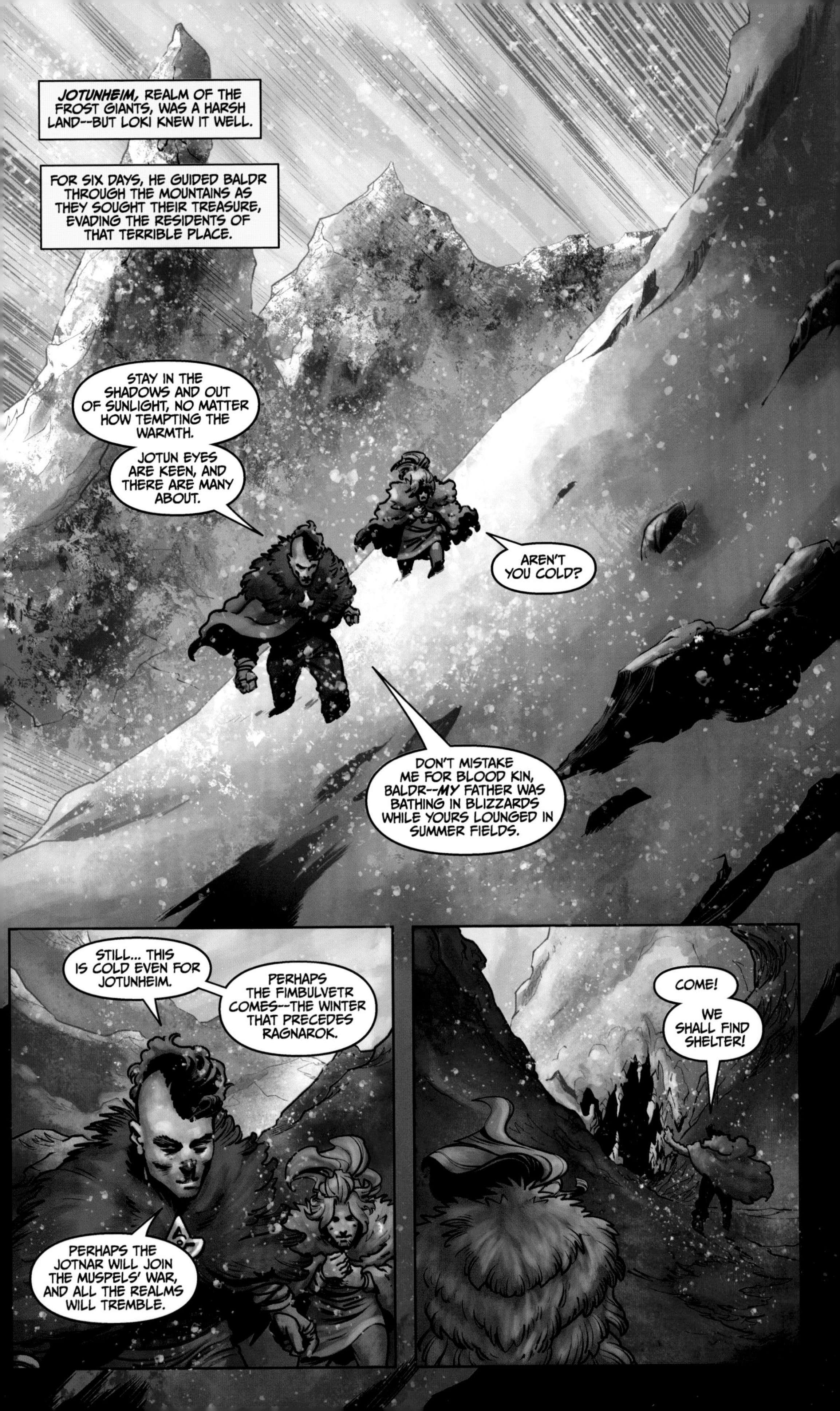
JOTUNHEIM, REALM OF THE FROST GIANTS, WAS A HARSH LAND--BUT LOKI KNEW IT WELL.
FOR SIX DAYS, HE GUIDED BALDR THROUGH THE MOUNTAINS AS THEY SOUGHT THEIR TREASURE, EVADING THE RESIDENTS OF THAT TERRIBLE PLACE.
STAY IN THE SHADOWS AND OUT OF SUNLIGHT, NO MATTER HOW TEMPTING THE WARMTH.
JOTUN EYES ARE KEEN, AND THERE ARE MANY ABOUT.
AREN'T YOU COLD?
DON'T MISTAKE ME FOR BLOOD KIN, BALDR--MY FATHER WAS BATHING IN BLIZZARDS WHILE YOURS LOUNGED IN SUMMER FIELDS.
STILL... THIS IS COLD EVEN FOR JOTUNHEIM.
PERHAPS THE FIMBULVETR COMES--THE WINTER THAT PRECEDES RAGNAROK.
PERHAPS THE JOTNAR WILL JOIN THE MUSPELS' WAR, AND ALL THE REALMS WILL TREMBLE.
COME!
WE SHALL FIND SHELTER!

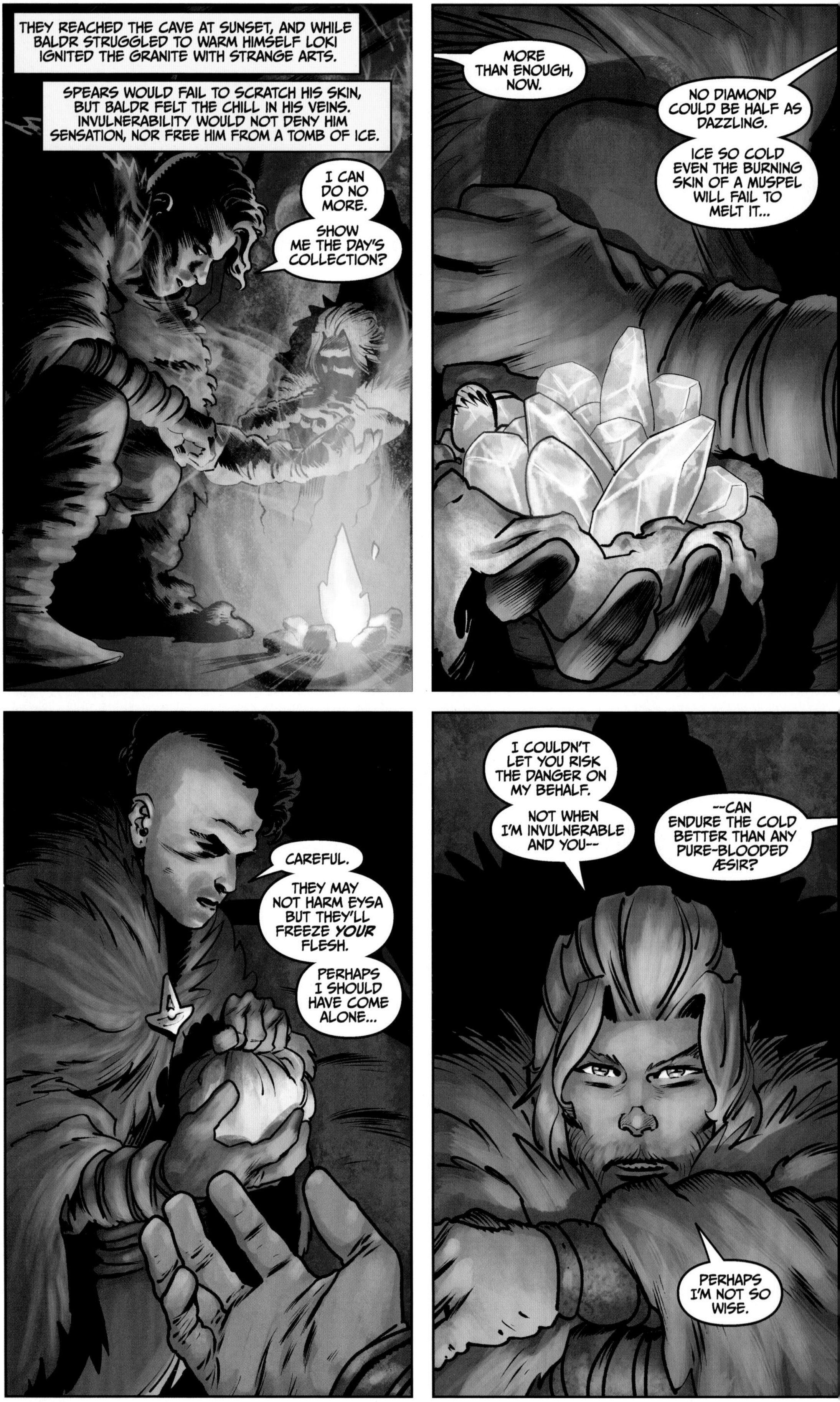
THEY REACHED THE CAVE AT SUNSET, AND WHILE BALDR STRUGGLED TO WARM HIMSELF LOKI IGNITED THE GRANITE WITH STRANGE ARTS.
SPEARS WOULD FAIL TO SCRATCH HIS SKIN, BUT BALDR FELT THE CHILL IN HIS VEINS. INVULNERABILITY WOULD NOT DENY HIM SENSATION, NOR FREE HIM FROM A TOMB OF ICE.
I CAN DO NO MORE.
SHOW ME THE DAY'S COLLECTION?
MORE THAN ENOUGH, NOW.
NO DIAMOND COULD BE HALF AS DAZZLING.
ICE SO COLD EVEN THE BURNING SKIN OF A MUSPEL WILL FAIL TO MELT IT...
CAREFUL.
THEY MAY NOT HARM EYSA BUT THEY'LL FREEZE ***YOUR*** FLESH.
PERHAPS I SHOULD HAVE COME ALONE...
I COULDN'T LET YOU RISK THE DANGER ON MY BEHALF.
NOT WHEN I'M INVULNERABLE AND YOU--
--CAN ENDURE THE COLD BETTER THAN ANY PURE-BLOODED ÆSIR?
PERHAPS I'M NOT SO WISE.

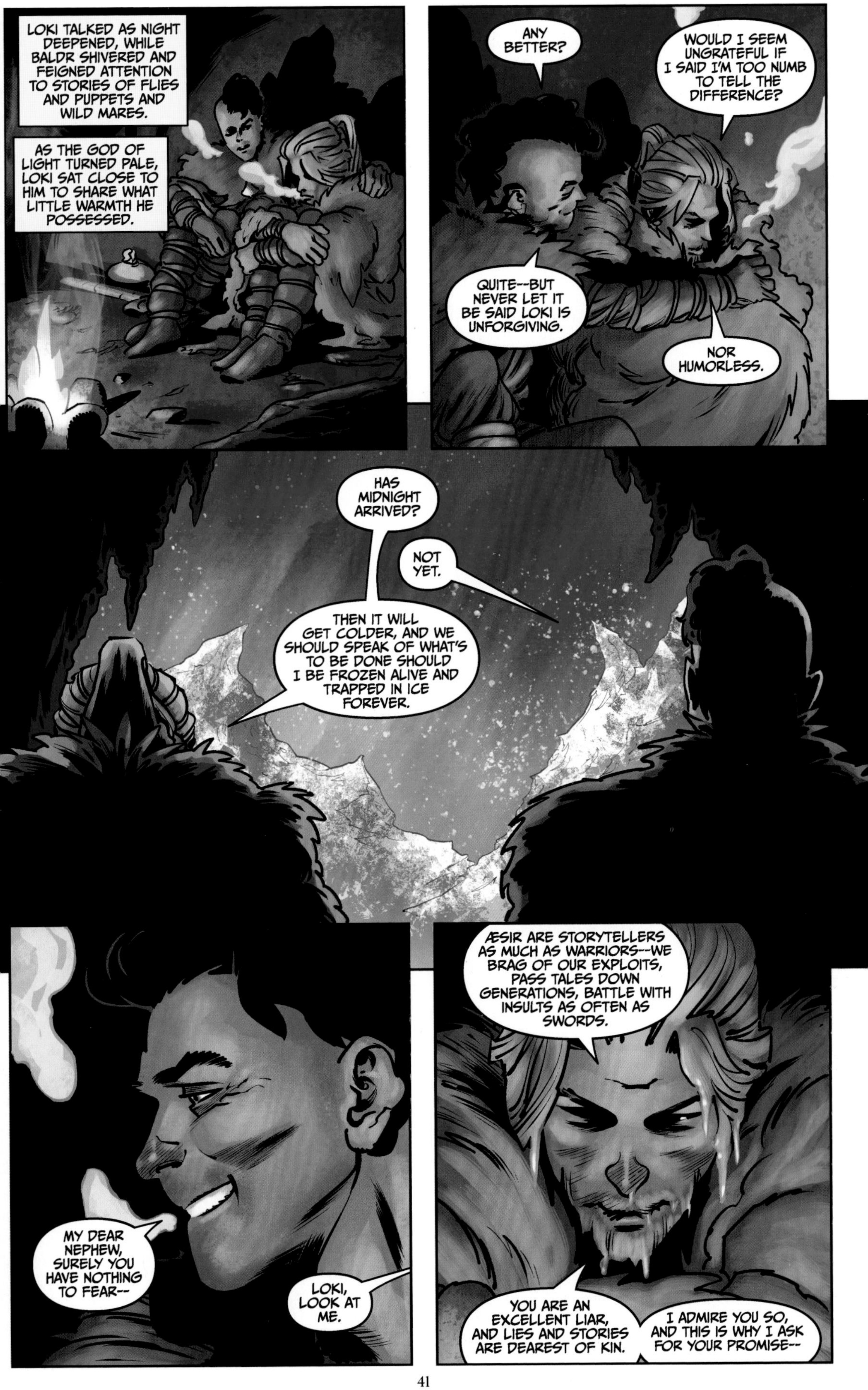
LOKI TALKED AS NIGHT DEEPENED, WHILE BALDR SHIVERED AND FEIGNED ATTENTION TO STORIES OF FLIES AND PUPPETS AND WILD MARES.
AS THE GOD OF LIGHT TURNED PALE, LOKI SAT CLOSE TO HIM TO SHARE WHAT LITTLE WARMTH HE POSSESSED.
ANY BETTER?
WOULD I SEEM UNGRATEFUL IF I SAID I'M TOO NUMB TO TELL THE DIFFERENCE?
QUITE--BUT NEVER LET IT BE SAID LOKI IS UNFORGIVING.
NOR HUMORLESS.
HAS MIDNIGHT ARRIVED?
NOT YET.
THEN IT WILL GET COLDER, AND WE SHOULD SPEAK OF WHAT'S TO BE DONE SHOULD I BE FROZEN ALIVE AND TRAPPED IN ICE FOREVER.
MY DEAR NEPHEW, SURELY YOU HAVE NOTHING TO FEAR--
LOKI, LOOK AT ME.
ÆSIR ARE STORYTELLERS AS MUCH AS WARRIORS--WE BRAG OF OUR EXPLOITS, PASS TALES DOWN GENERATIONS, BATTLE WITH INSULTS AS OFTEN AS SWORDS.
YOU ARE AN EXCELLENT LIAR, AND LIES AND STORIES ARE DEAREST OF KIN.
I ADMIRE YOU SO, AND THIS IS WHY I ASK FOR YOUR PROMISE--

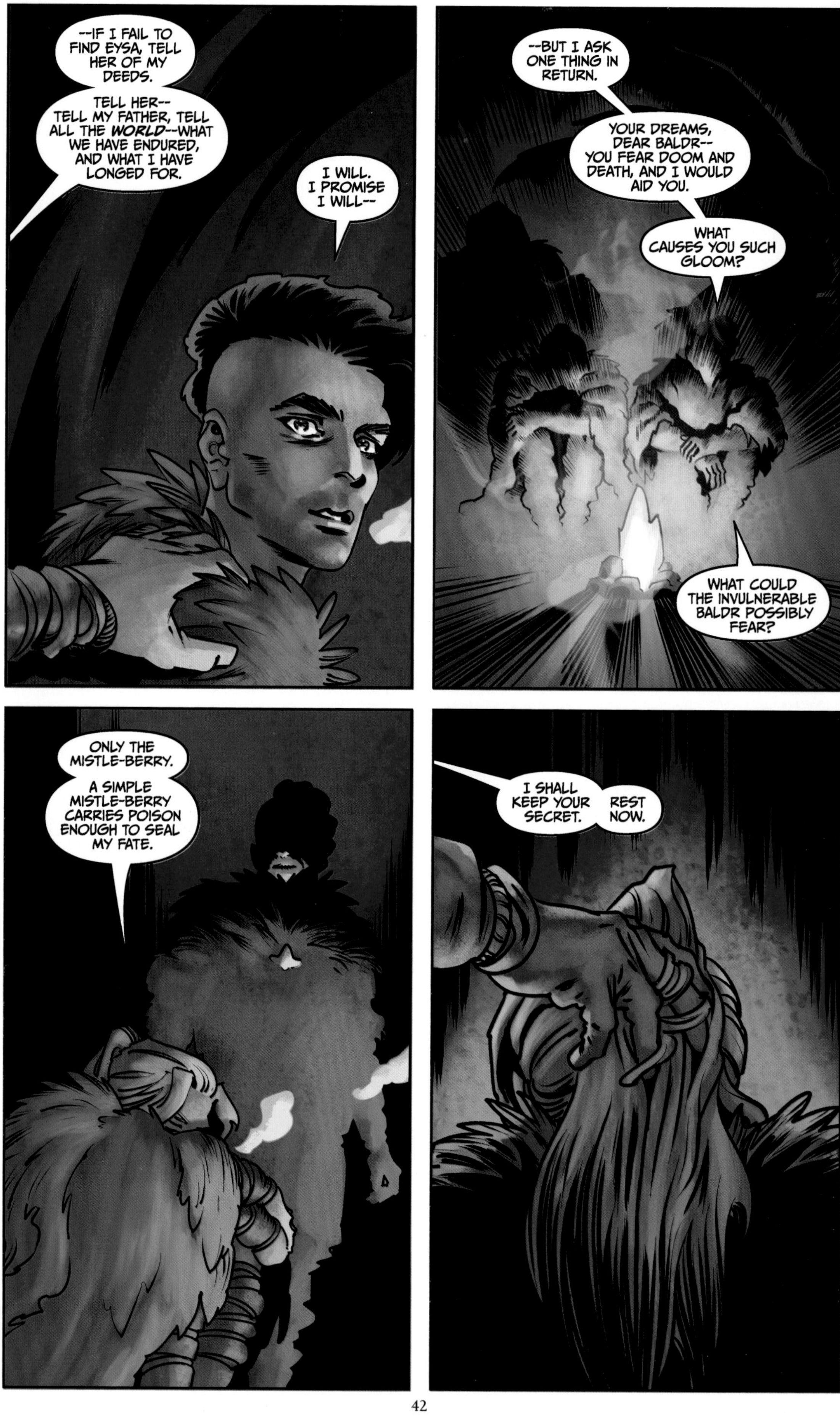
--IF I FAIL TO FIND EYSA, TELL HER OF MY DEEDS.
TELL HER-- TELL MY FATHER, TELL ALL THE *WORLD*--WHAT WE HAVE ENDURED, AND WHAT I HAVE LONGED FOR.
I WILL. I PROMISE I WILL--
--BUT I ASK ONE THING IN RETURN.
YOUR DREAMS, DEAR BALDR-- YOU FEAR DOOM AND DEATH, AND I WOULD AID YOU.
WHAT CAUSES YOU SUCH GLOOM?
WHAT COULD THE INVULNERABLE BALDR POSSIBLY FEAR?
ONLY THE MISTLE-BERRY.
A SIMPLE MISTLE-BERRY CARRIES POISON ENOUGH TO SEAL MY FATE.
I SHALL KEEP YOUR SECRET.
REST NOW.

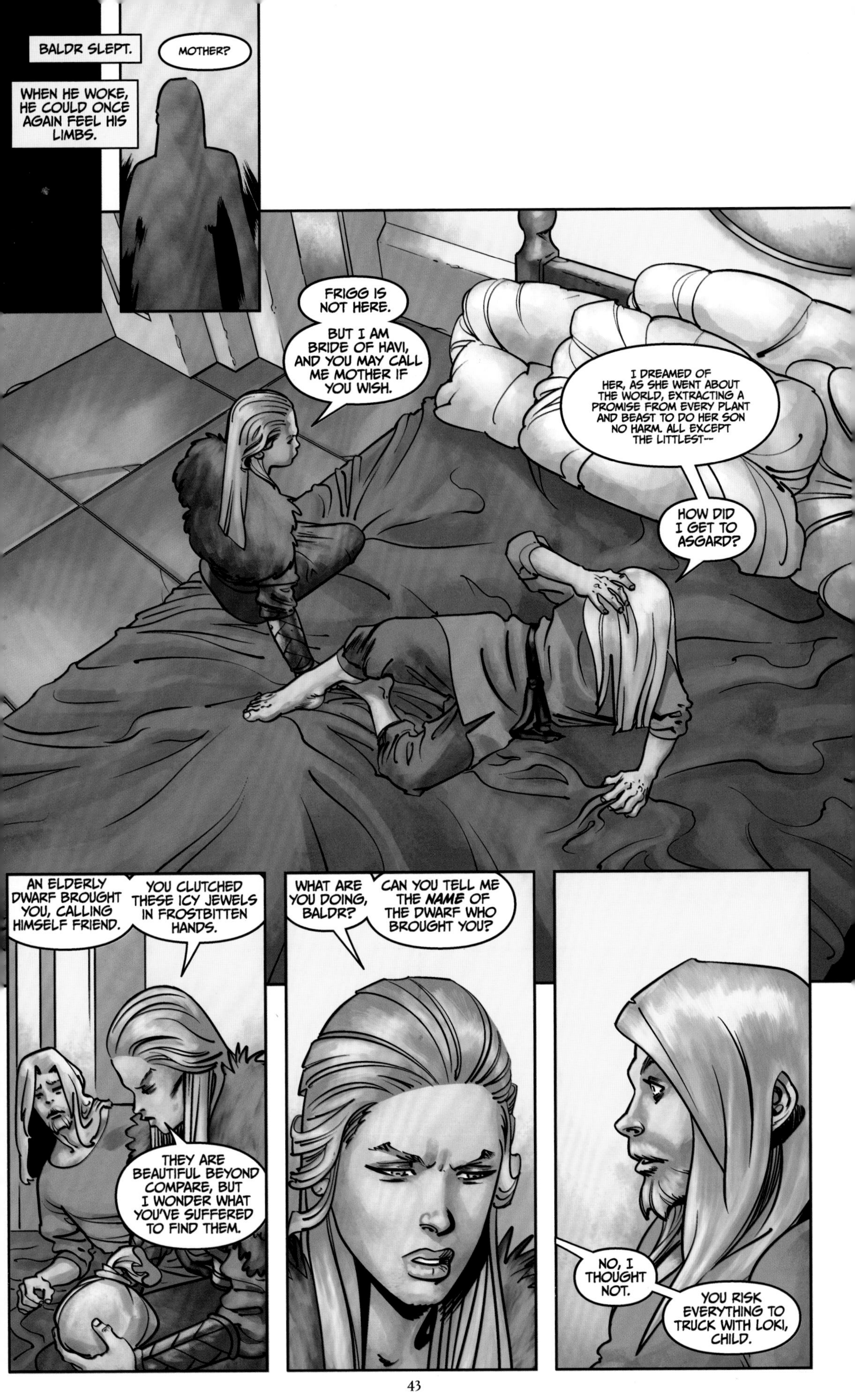
BALDR SLEPT.
MOTHER?
WHEN HE WOKE, HE COULD ONCE AGAIN FEEL HIS LIMBS.
FRIGG IS NOT HERE.
BUT I AM BRIDE OF HAVI, AND YOU MAY CALL ME MOTHER IF YOU WISH.
I DREAMED OF HER, AS SHE WENT ABOUT THE WORLD, EXTRACTING A PROMISE FROM EVERY PLANT AND BEAST TO DO HER SON NO HARM. ALL EXCEPT THE LITTLEST--
HOW DID I GET TO ASGARD?
AN ELDERLY DWARF BROUGHT YOU, CALLING HIMSELF FRIEND.
YOU CLUTCHED THESE ICY JEWELS IN FROSTBITTEN HANDS.
THEY ARE BEAUTIFUL BEYOND COMPARE, BUT I WONDER WHAT YOU'VE SUFFERED TO FIND THEM.
WHAT ARE YOU DOING, BALDR?
CAN YOU TELL ME THE ***NAME*** OF THE DWARF WHO BROUGHT YOU?
NO, I THOUGHT NOT.
YOU RISK EVERYTHING TO TRUCK WITH LOKI, CHILD.

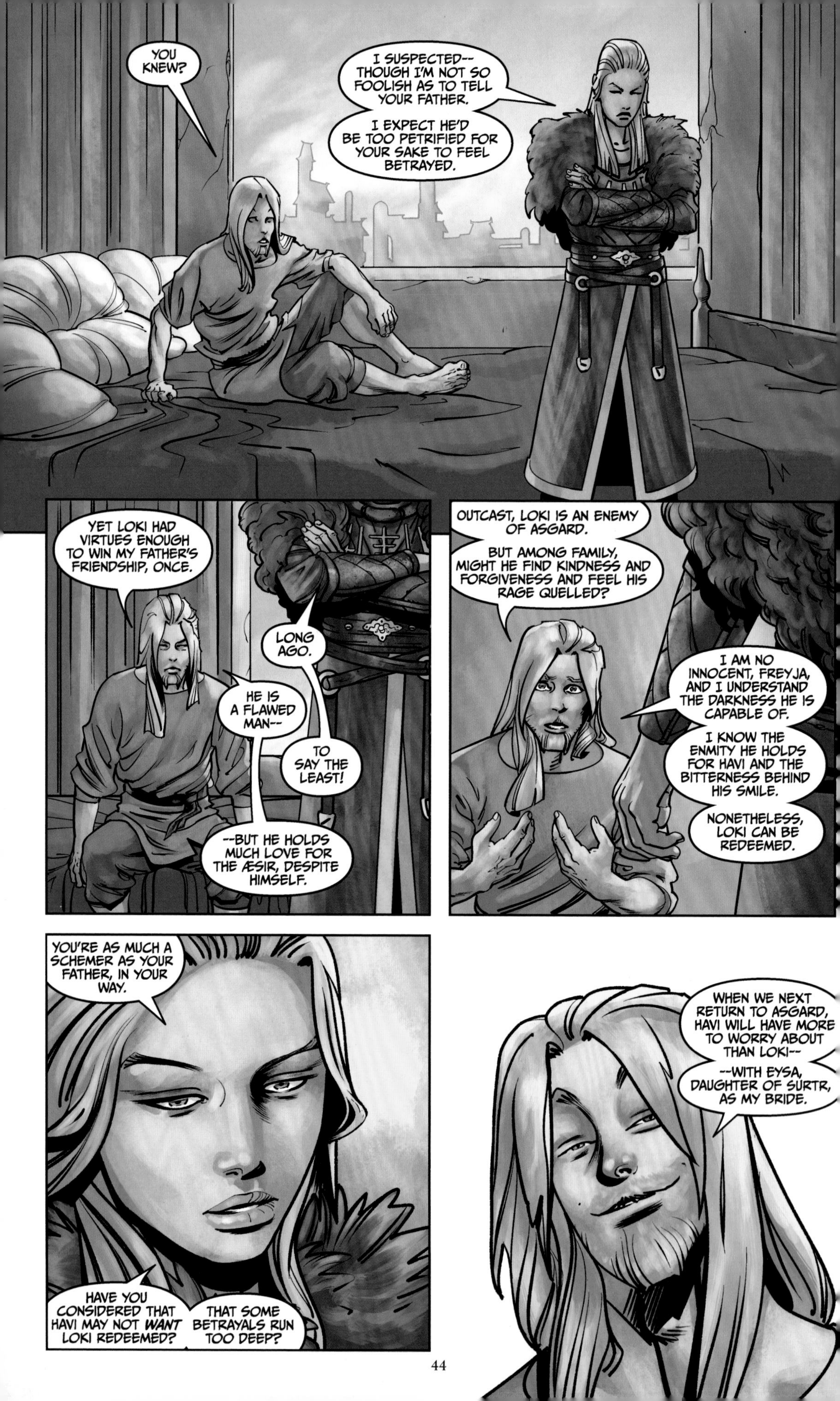
YOU KNEW?
I SUSPECTED-- THOUGH I'M NOT SO FOOLISH AS TO TELL YOUR FATHER.
I EXPECT HE'D BE TOO PETRIFIED FOR YOUR SAKE TO FEEL BETRAYED.
YET LOKI HAD VIRTUES ENOUGH TO WIN MY FATHER'S FRIENDSHIP, ONCE.
LONG AGO.
HE IS A FLAWED MAN--
TO SAY THE LEAST!
--BUT HE HOLDS MUCH LOVE FOR THE ÆSIR, DESPITE HIMSELF.
OUTCAST, LOKI IS AN ENEMY OF ASGARD.
BUT AMONG FAMILY, MIGHT HE FIND KINDNESS AND FORGIVENESS AND FEEL HIS RAGE QUELLED?
I AM NO INNOCENT, FREYJA, AND I UNDERSTAND THE DARKNESS HE IS CAPABLE OF.
I KNOW THE ENMITY HE HOLDS FOR HAVI AND THE BITTERNESS BEHIND HIS SMILE.
NONETHELESS, LOKI CAN BE REDEEMED.
YOU'RE AS MUCH A SCHEMER AS YOUR FATHER, IN YOUR WAY.
HAVE YOU CONSIDERED THAT HAVI MAY NOT *WANT* LOKI REDEEMED?
THAT SOME BETRAYALS RUN TOO DEEP?
WHEN WE NEXT RETURN TO ASGARD, HAVI WILL HAVE MORE TO WORRY ABOUT THAN LOKI--
--WITH EYSA, DAUGHTER OF SURTR, AS MY BRIDE.

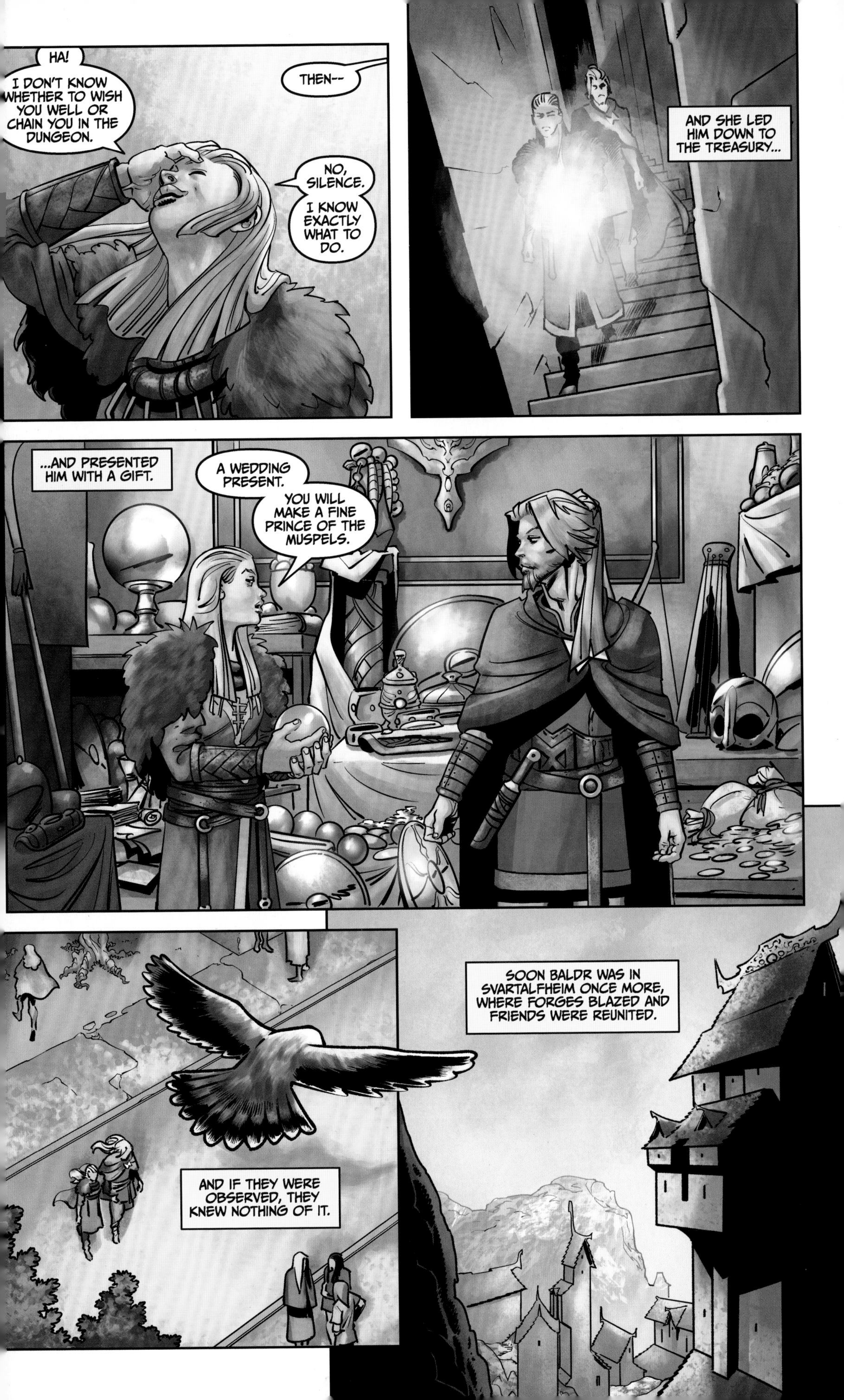
HA!
I DON'T KNOW WHETHER TO WISH YOU WELL OR CHAIN YOU IN THE DUNGEON.
THEN--
NO, SILENCE.
I KNOW EXACTLY WHAT TO DO.
AND SHE LED HIM DOWN TO THE TREASURY...
...AND PRESENTED HIM WITH A GIFT.
A WEDDING PRESENT.
YOU WILL MAKE A FINE PRINCE OF THE MUSPELS.
AND IF THEY WERE OBSERVED, THEY KNEW NOTHING OF IT.
SOON BALDR WAS IN SVARTALFHEIM ONCE MORE, WHERE FORGES BLAZED AND FRIENDS WERE REUNITED.

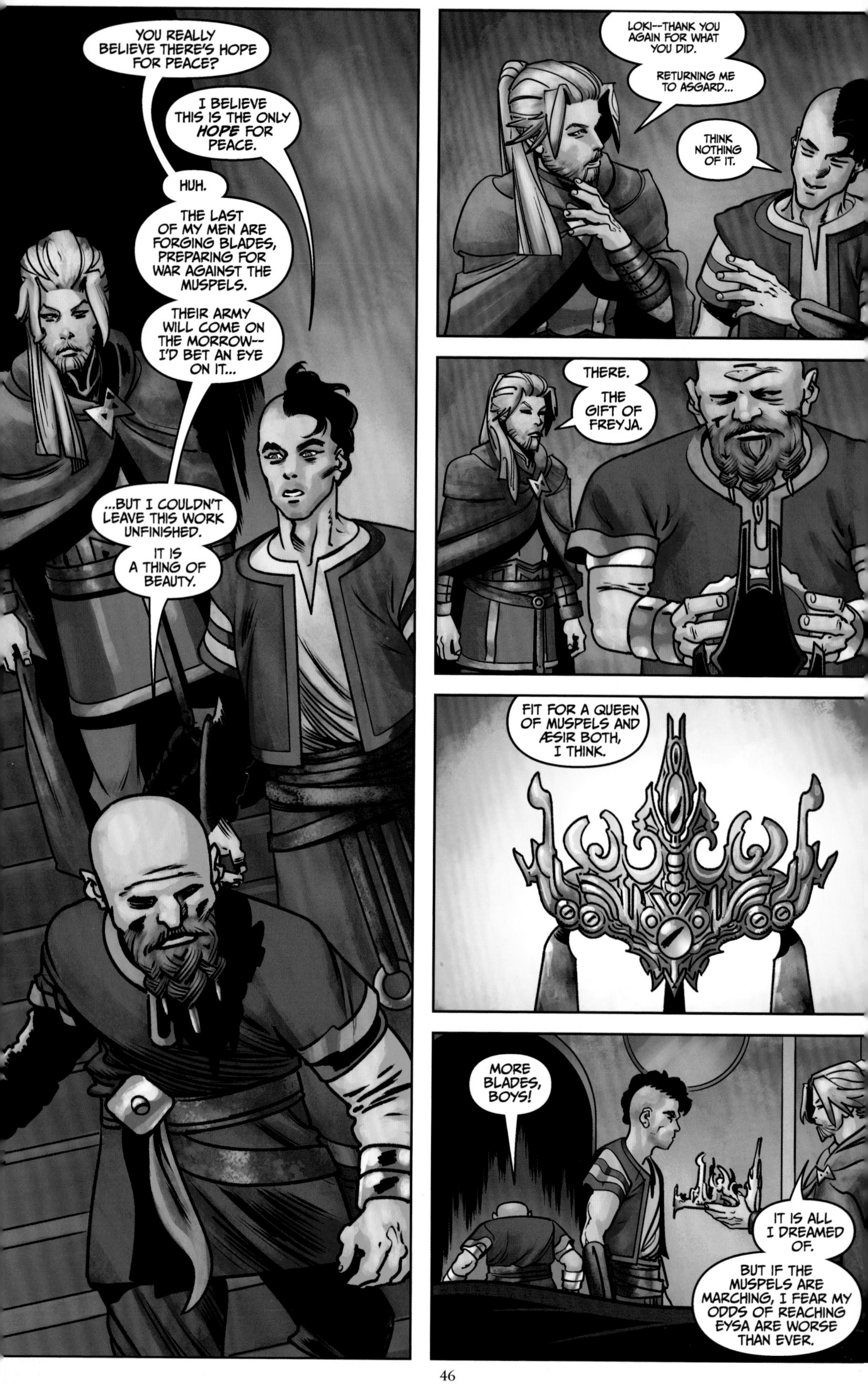
YOU REALLY BELIEVE THERE'S HOPE FOR PEACE?
I BELIEVE THIS IS THE ONLY *HOPE* FOR PEACE.
HUH.
THE LAST OF MY MEN ARE FORGING BLADES, PREPARING FOR WAR AGAINST THE MUSPELS.
THEIR ARMY WILL COME ON THE MORROW-- I'D BET AN EYE ON IT...
...BUT I COULDN'T LEAVE THIS WORK UNFINISHED.
IT IS A THING OF BEAUTY.
LOKI--THANK YOU AGAIN FOR WHAT YOU DID.
RETURNING ME TO ASGARD...
THINK NOTHING OF IT.
THERE.
THE GIFT OF FREYJA.
FIT FOR A QUEEN OF MUSPELS AND ÆSIR BOTH, I THINK.
MORE BLADES, BOYS!
IT IS ALL I DREAMED OF.
BUT IF THE MUSPELS ARE MARCHING, I FEAR MY ODDS OF REACHING EYSA ARE WORSE THAN EVER.

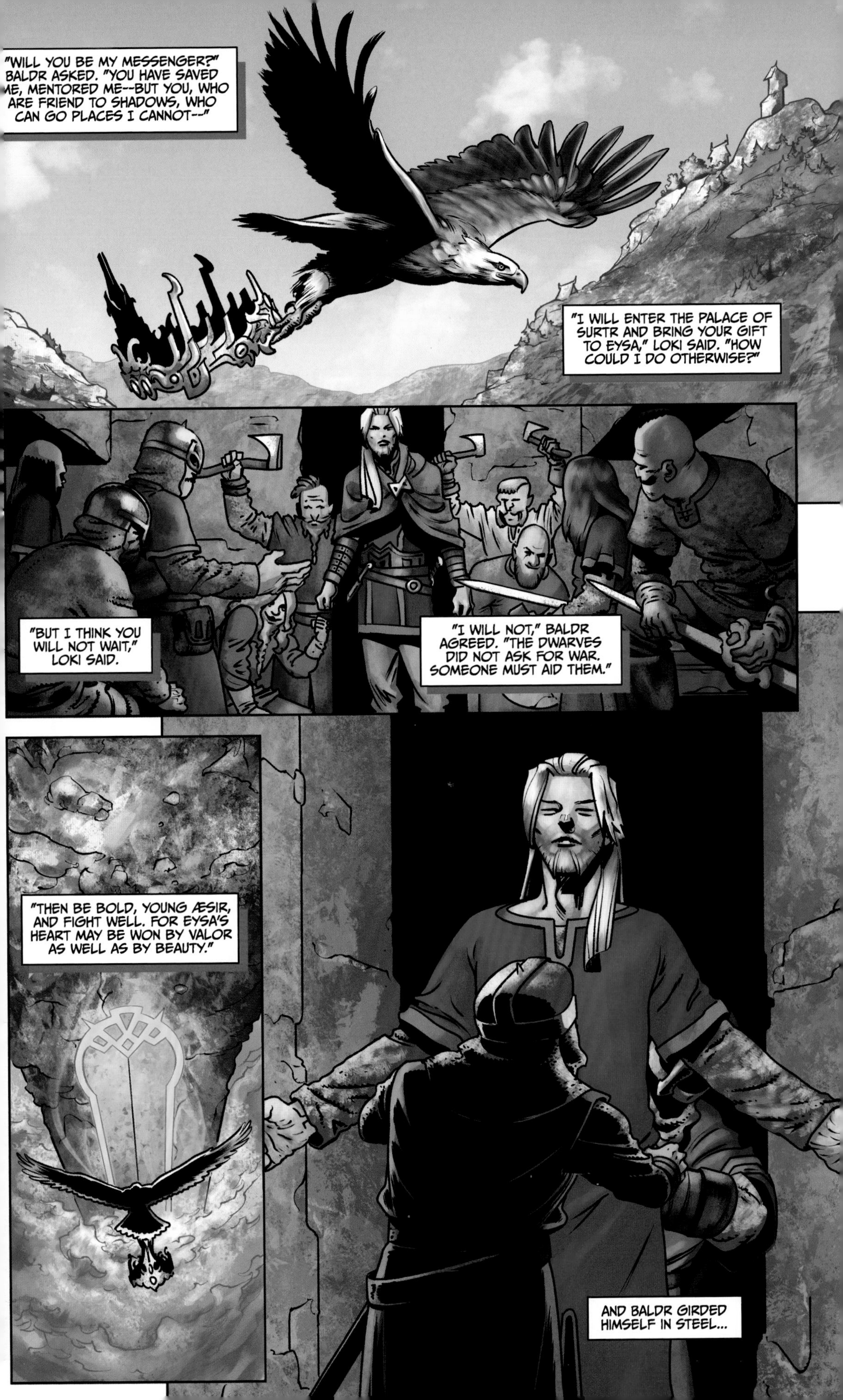
"WILL YOU BE MY MESSENGER?" BALDR ASKED. "YOU HAVE SAVED ME, MENTORED ME--BUT YOU, WHO ARE FRIEND TO SHADOWS, WHO CAN GO PLACES I CANNOT--"
"I WILL ENTER THE PALACE OF SURTR AND BRING YOUR GIFT TO EYSA," LOKI SAID. "HOW COULD I DO OTHERWISE?"
"BUT I THINK YOU WILL NOT WAIT," LOKI SAID.
"I WILL NOT," BALDR AGREED. "THE DWARVES DID NOT ASK FOR WAR. SOMEONE MUST AID THEM."
"THEN BE BOLD, YOUNG ÆSIR, AND FIGHT WELL. FOR EYSA'S HEART MAY BE WON BY VALOR AS WELL AS BY BEAUTY."
AND BALDR GIRDED HIMSELF IN STEEL...

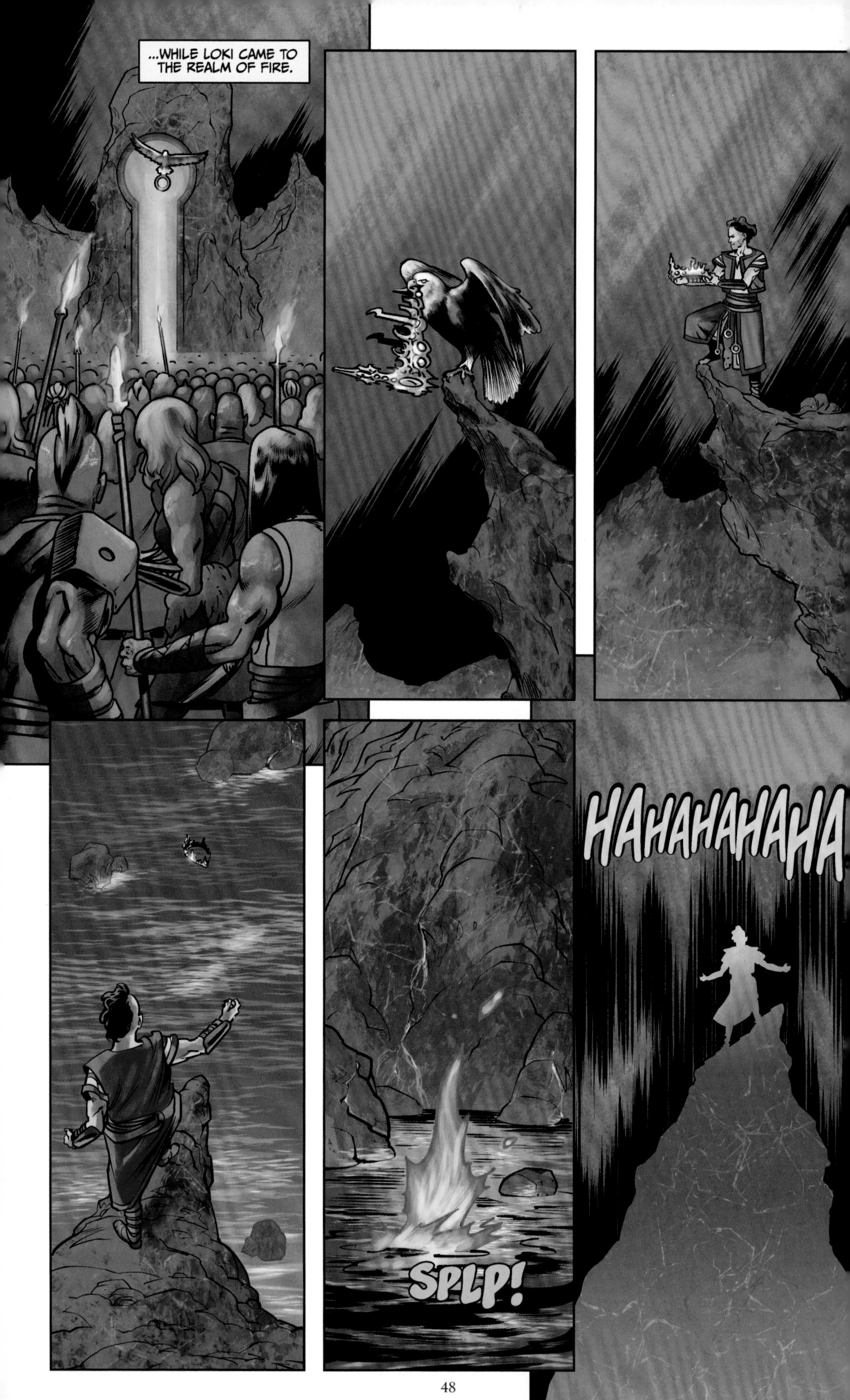
...WHILE LOKI CAME TO THE REALM OF FIRE.
SPLP!
HAHAHAHAHAHA

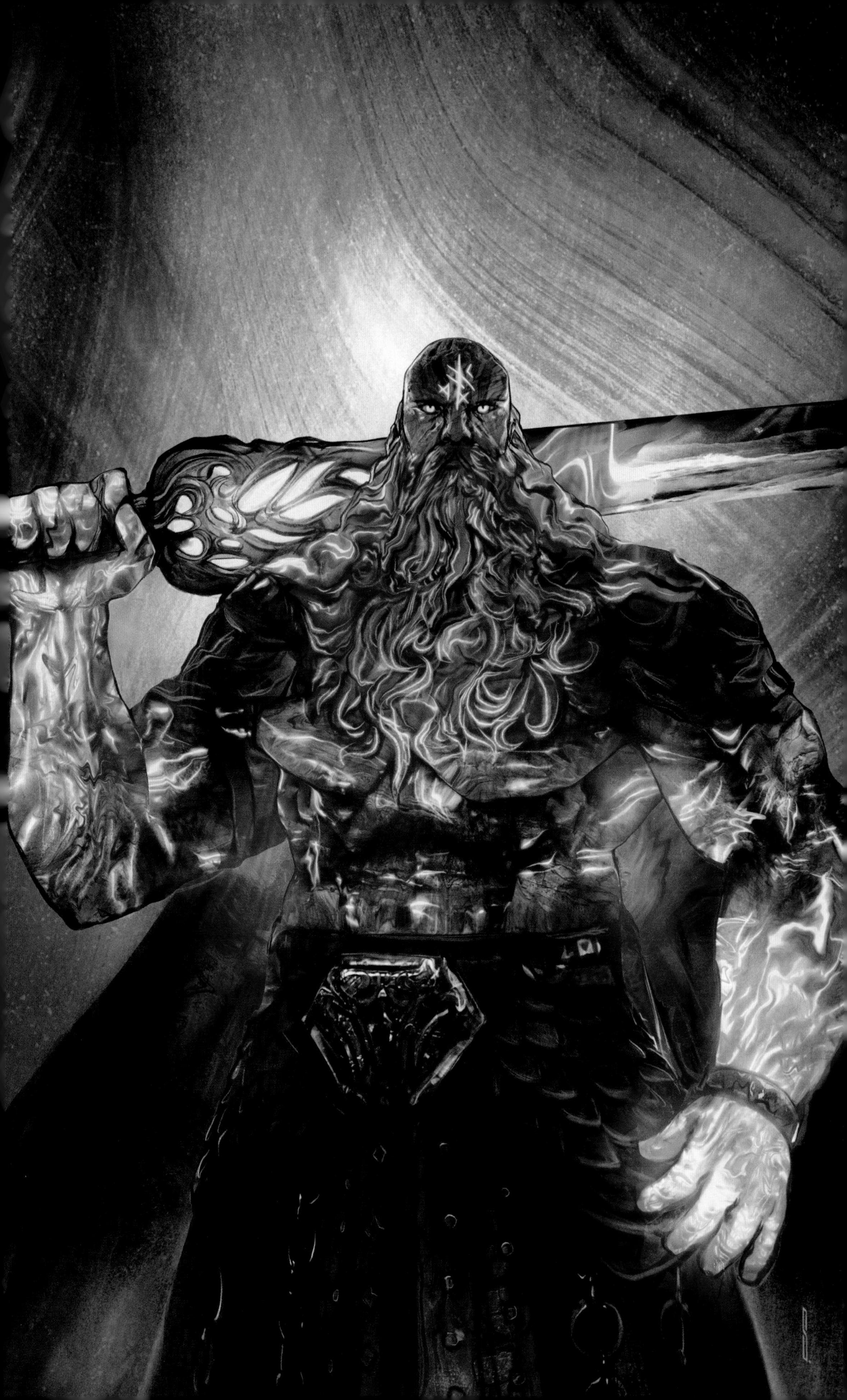

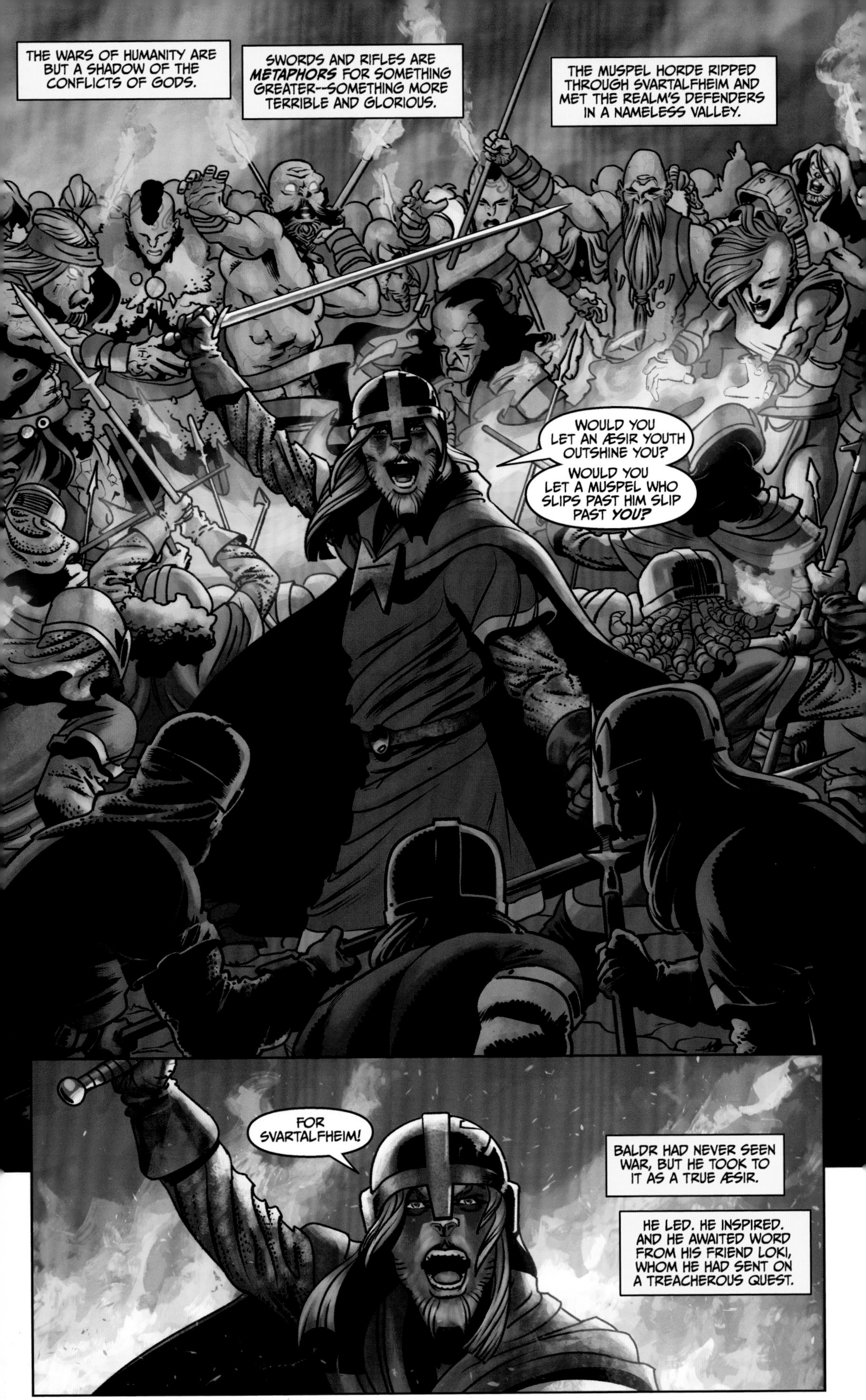
THE WARS OF HUMANITY ARE BUT A SHADOW OF THE CONFLICTS OF GODS.
SWORDS AND RIFLES ARE ***METAPHORS*** FOR SOMETHING GREATER--SOMETHING MORE TERRIBLE AND GLORIOUS.
THE MUSPEL HORDE RIPPED THROUGH SVARTALFHEIM AND MET THE REALM'S DEFENDERS IN A NAMELESS VALLEY.
WOULD YOU LET AN ÆSIR YOUTH OUTSHINE YOU?
WOULD YOU LET A MUSPEL WHO SLIPS PAST HIM SLIP PAST ***YOU?***
FOR SVARTALFHEIM!
BALDR HAD NEVER SEEN WAR, BUT HE TOOK TO IT AS A TRUE ÆSIR.
HE LED. HE INSPIRED. AND HE AWAITED WORD FROM HIS FRIEND LOKI, WHOM HE HAD SENT ON A TREACHEROUS QUEST.

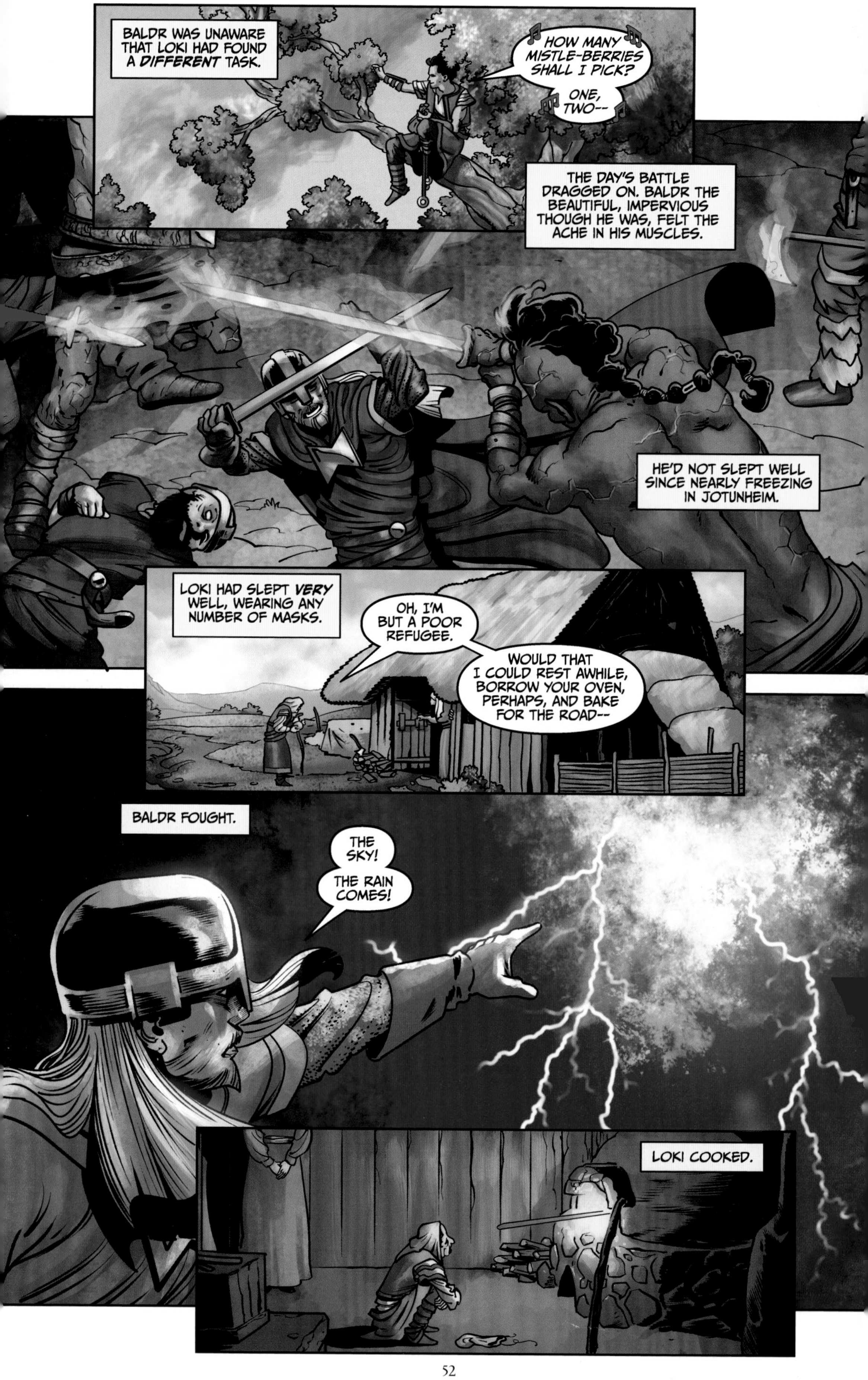
BALDR WAS UNAWARE THAT LOKI HAD FOUND A *DIFFERENT* TASK.
HOW MANY MISTLE-BERRIES SHALL I PICK?
ONE, TWO--
THE DAY'S BATTLE DRAGGED ON. BALDR THE BEAUTIFUL, IMPERVIOUS THOUGH HE WAS, FELT THE ACHE IN HIS MUSCLES.
HE'D NOT SLEPT WELL SINCE NEARLY FREEZING IN JOTUNHEIM.
LOKI HAD SLEPT *VERY* WELL, WEARING ANY NUMBER OF MASKS.
OH, I'M BUT A POOR REFUGEE.
WOULD THAT I COULD REST AWHILE, BORROW YOUR OVEN, PERHAPS, AND BAKE FOR THE ROAD--
BALDR FOUGHT.
THE SKY!
THE RAIN COMES!
LOKI COOKED.

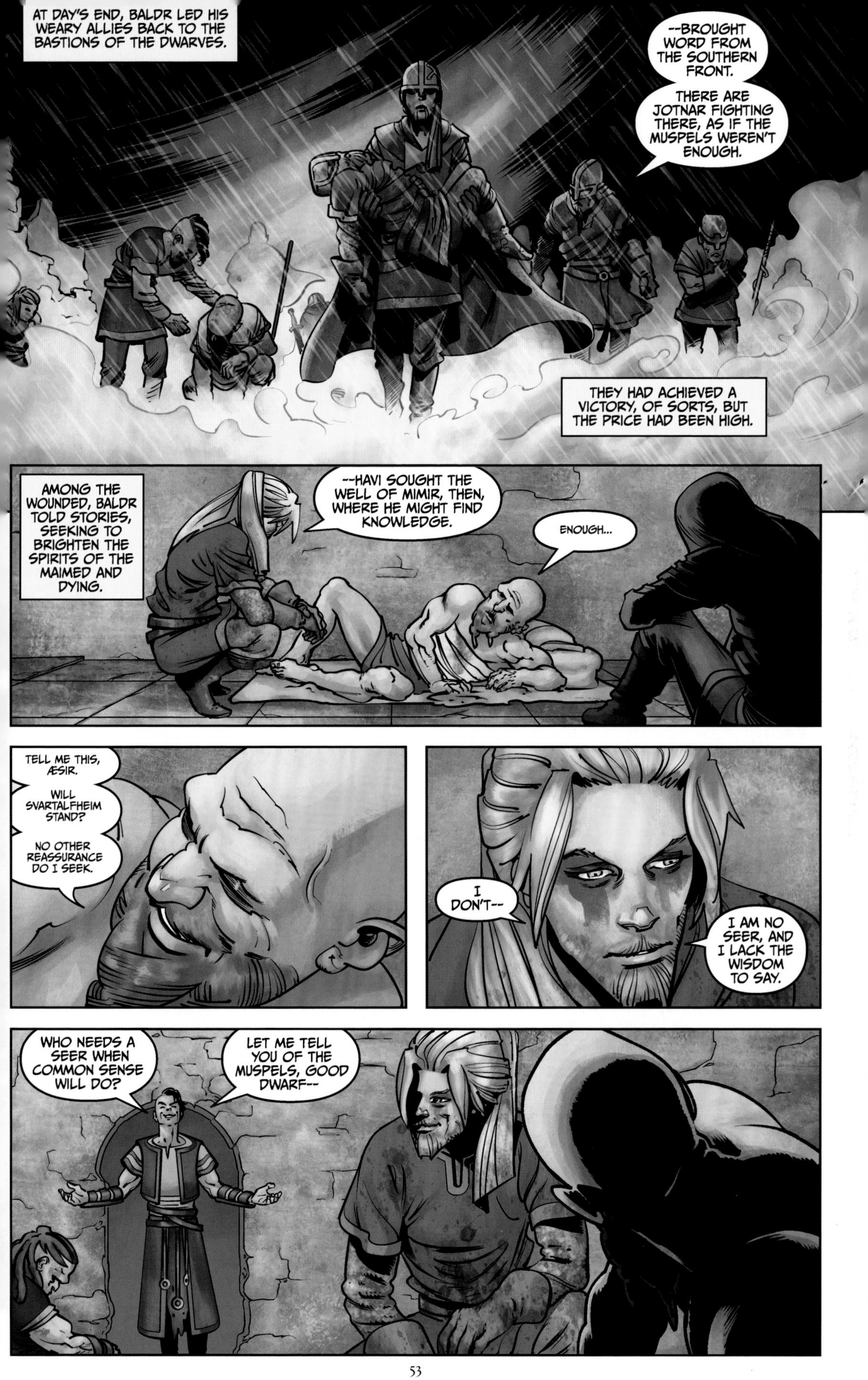
AT DAY'S END, BALDR LED HIS WEARY ALLIES BACK TO THE BASTIONS OF THE DWARVES.
--BROUGHT WORD FROM THE SOUTHERN FRONT.
THERE ARE JOTNAR FIGHTING THERE, AS IF THE MUSPELS WEREN'T ENOUGH.
THEY HAD ACHIEVED A VICTORY, OF SORTS, BUT THE PRICE HAD BEEN HIGH.
AMONG THE WOUNDED, BALDR TOLD STORIES, SEEKING TO BRIGHTEN THE SPIRITS OF THE MAIMED AND DYING.
--HAVI SOUGHT THE WELL OF MIMIR, THEN, WHERE HE MIGHT FIND KNOWLEDGE.
ENOUGH...
TELL ME THIS, ÆSIR.
WILL SVARTALFHEIM STAND?
NO OTHER REASSURANCE DO I SEEK.
I DON'T--
I AM NO SEER, AND I LACK THE WISDOM TO SAY.
WHO NEEDS A SEER WHEN COMMON SENSE WILL DO?
LET ME TELL YOU OF THE MUSPELS, GOOD DWARF--

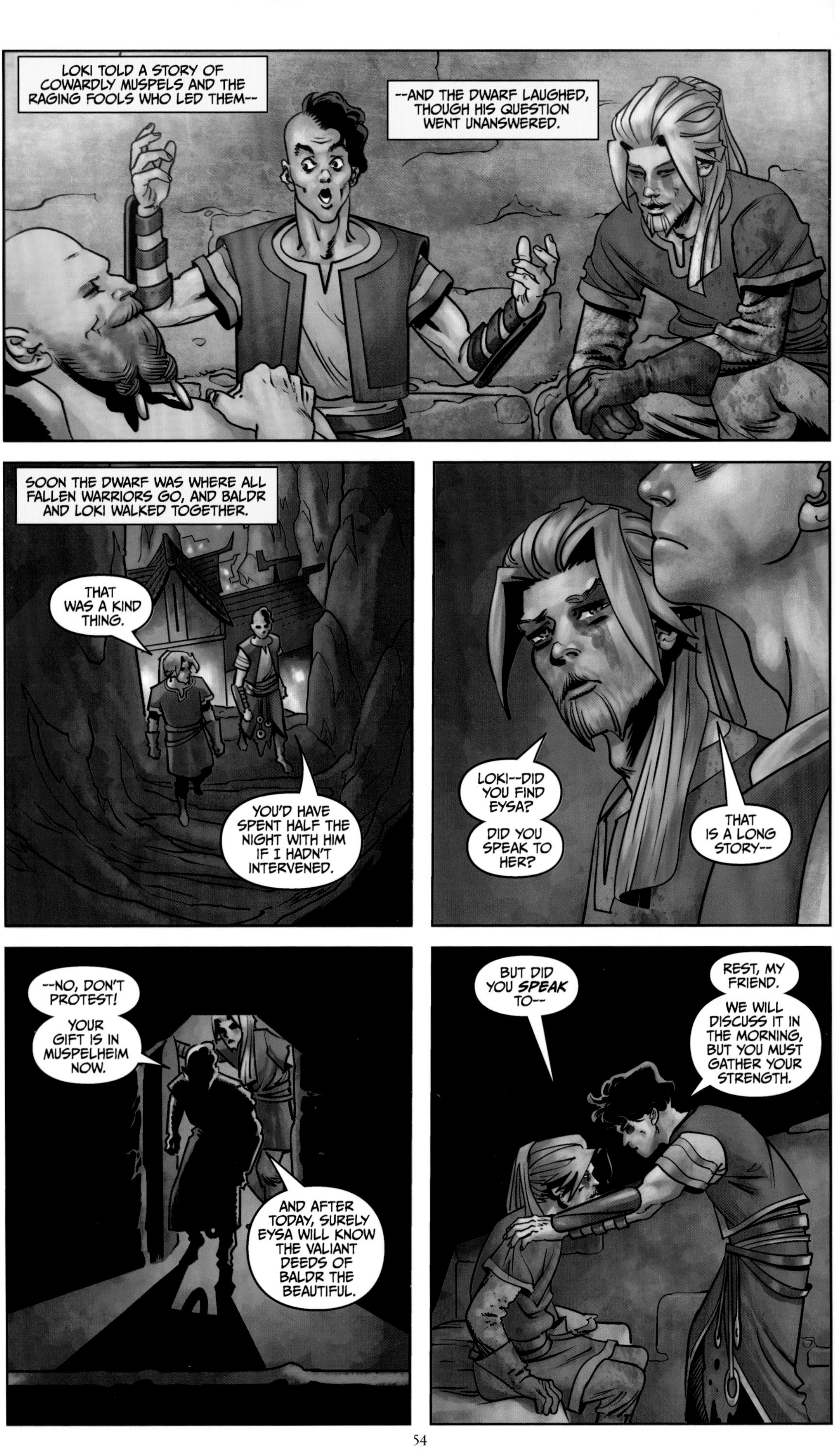
LOKI TOLD A STORY OF COWARDLY MUSPELS AND THE RAGING FOOLS WHO LED THEM--
--AND THE DWARF LAUGHED, THOUGH HIS QUESTION WENT UNANSWERED.
SOON THE DWARF WAS WHERE ALL FALLEN WARRIORS GO, AND BALDR AND LOKI WALKED TOGETHER.
THAT WAS A KIND THING.
YOU'D HAVE SPENT HALF THE NIGHT WITH HIM IF I HADN'T INTERVENED.
LOKI--DID YOU FIND EYSA?
DID YOU SPEAK TO HER?
THAT IS A LONG STORY--
--NO, DON'T PROTEST!
YOUR GIFT IS IN MUSPELHEIM NOW.
AND AFTER TODAY, SURELY EYSA WILL KNOW THE VALIANT DEEDS OF BALDR THE BEAUTIFUL.
BUT DID YOU SPEAK TO--
REST, MY FRIEND.
WE WILL DISCUSS IT IN THE MORNING, BUT YOU MUST GATHER YOUR STRENGTH.

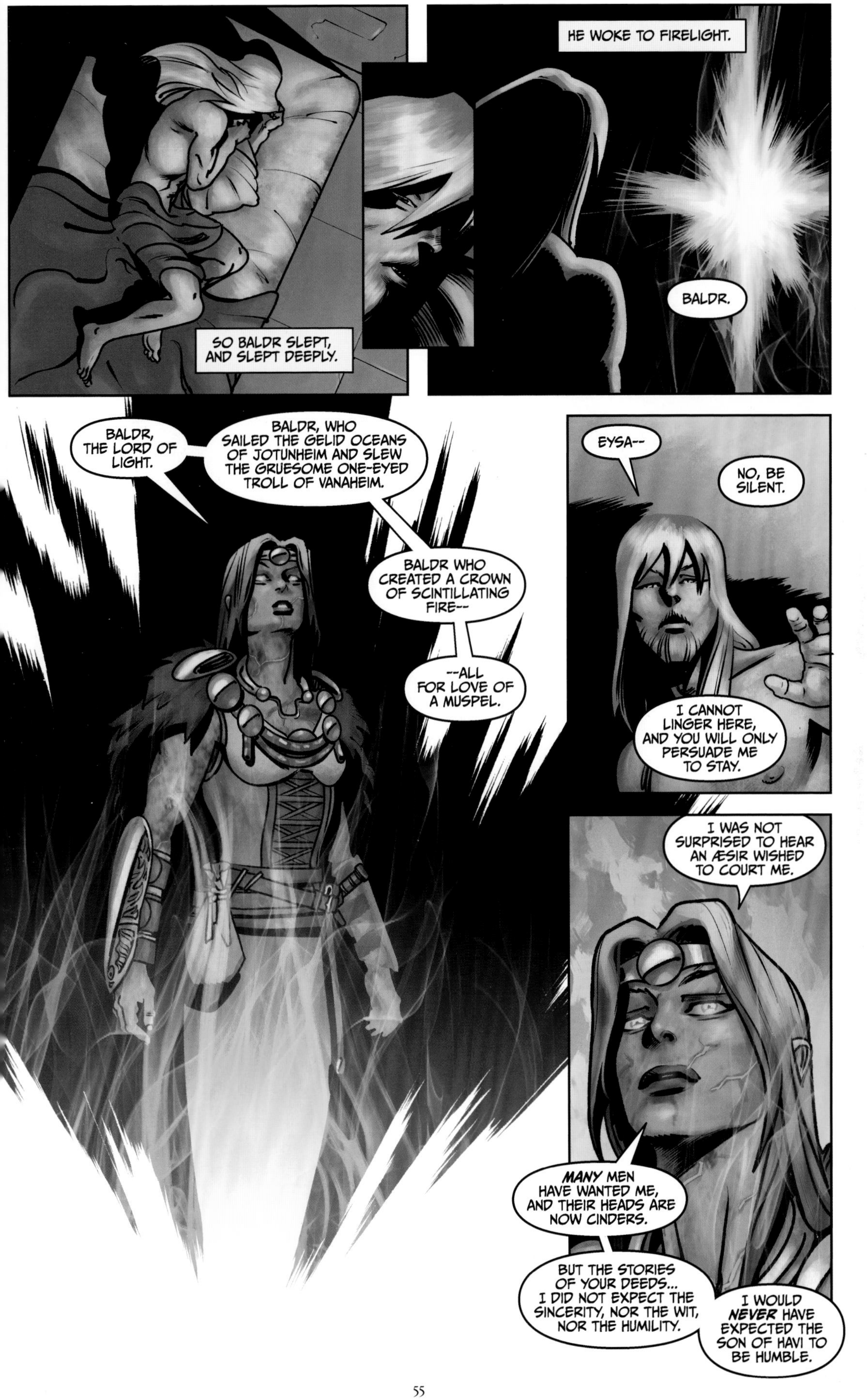

SO BALDR SLEPT, AND SLEPT DEEPLY.
HE WOKE TO FIRELIGHT.
BALDR.
BALDR, THE LORD OF LIGHT.
BALDR, WHO SAILED THE GELID OCEANS OF JOTUNHEIM AND SLEW THE GRUESOME ONE-EYED TROLL OF VANAHEIM.
BALDR WHO CREATED A CROWN OF SCINTILLATING FIRE--
--ALL FOR LOVE OF A MUSPEL.
EYSA--
NO, BE SILENT.
I CANNOT LINGER HERE, AND YOU WILL ONLY PERSUADE ME TO STAY.
I WAS NOT SURPRISED TO HEAR AN ÆSIR WISHED TO COURT ME.
MANY MEN HAVE WANTED ME, AND THEIR HEADS ARE NOW CINDERS.
BUT THE STORIES OF YOUR DEEDS... I DID NOT EXPECT THE SINCERITY, NOR THE WIT, NOR THE HUMILITY.
I WOULD ***NEVER*** HAVE EXPECTED THE SON OF HAVI TO BE HUMBLE.

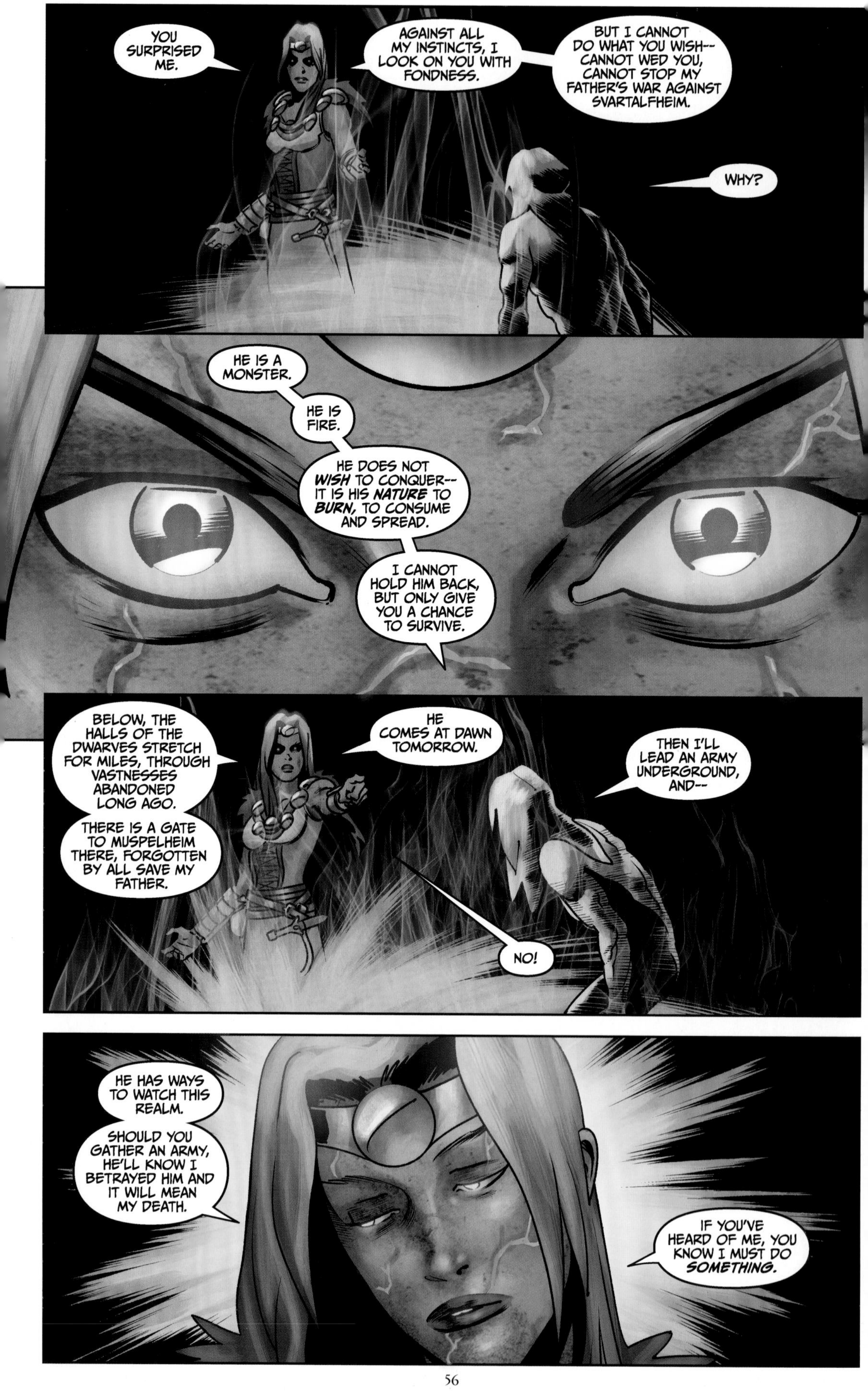
YOU SURPRISED ME.
AGAINST ALL MY INSTINCTS, I LOOK ON YOU WITH FONDNESS.
BUT I CANNOT DO WHAT YOU WISH-- CANNOT WED YOU, CANNOT STOP MY FATHER'S WAR AGAINST SVARTALFHEIM.
WHY?
HE IS A MONSTER.
HE IS FIRE.
HE DOES NOT WISH TO CONQUER-- IT IS HIS NATURE TO BURN, TO CONSUME AND SPREAD.
I CANNOT HOLD HIM BACK, BUT ONLY GIVE YOU A CHANCE TO SURVIVE.
BELOW, THE HALLS OF THE DWARVES STRETCH FOR MILES, THROUGH VASTNESSES ABANDONED LONG AGO.
THERE IS A GATE TO MUSPELHEIM THERE, FORGOTTEN BY ALL SAVE MY FATHER.
HE COMES AT DAWN TOMORROW.
THEN I'LL LEAD AN ARMY UNDERGROUND, AND--
NO!
HE HAS WAYS TO WATCH THIS REALM.
SHOULD YOU GATHER AN ARMY, HE'LL KNOW I BETRAYED HIM AND IT WILL MEAN MY DEATH.
IF YOU'VE HEARD OF ME, YOU KNOW I MUST DO SOMETHING.

THE DWARVES ARE DOOMED ANYWAY.

RETURN TO ASGARD, BALDR-- PREPARE FOR WAR THERE.

ASSEMBLE A GRANDER ARMY THAN THIS LOT AND RIDE TO VICTORY, LEADING YOUR ÆSIR LIKE A STORM.

WHEN MY FATHER IS DEAD AT YOUR HAND, THEN WE MAY WED--AS IS THE MUSPEL WAY.

MUST IT BE SO BLOODY?

THAT IS THE PRICE OF PEACE AMONG MY KIND.

BUT I CAN OFFER A TOKEN OF MY ADORATION--THE ONLY THING I HAD TIME TO PREPARE.

A CAKE, TO GIVE YOU STRENGTH FOR YOUR JOURNEY.

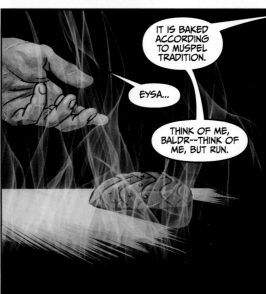

IT IS BAKED ACCORDING TO MUSPEL TRADITION.

EYSA...

THINK OF ME, BALDR--THINK OF ME, BUT RUN.

EYSA?

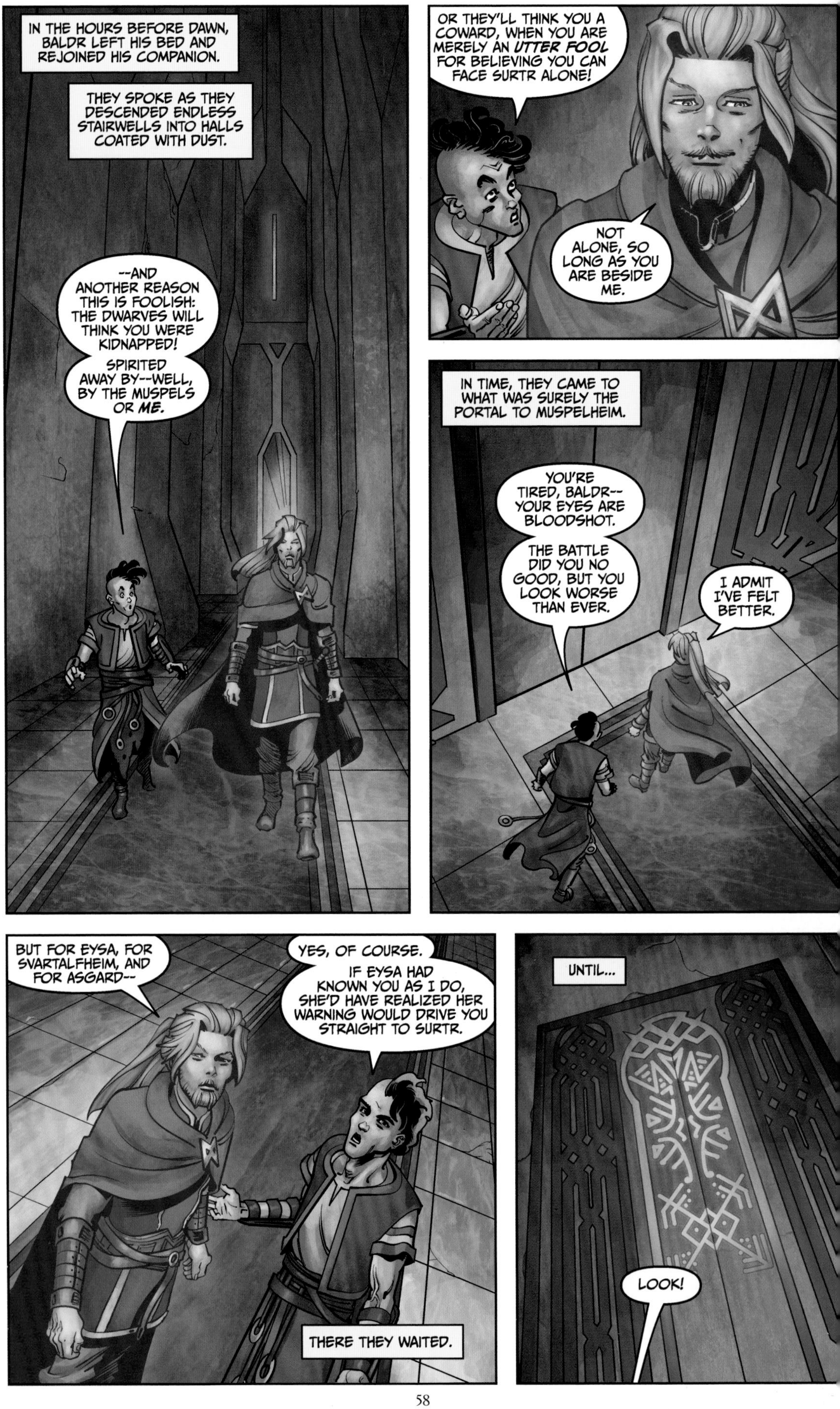
IN THE HOURS BEFORE DAWN, BALDR LEFT HIS BED AND REJOINED HIS COMPANION.
THEY SPOKE AS THEY DESCENDED ENDLESS STAIRWELLS INTO HALLS COATED WITH DUST.
--AND ANOTHER REASON THIS IS FOOLISH: THE DWARVES WILL THINK YOU WERE KIDNAPPED!
SPIRITED AWAY BY--WELL, BY THE MUSPELS OR *ME.*
OR THEY'LL THINK YOU A COWARD, WHEN YOU ARE MERELY AN *UTTER FOOL* FOR BELIEVING YOU CAN FACE SURTR ALONE!
NOT ALONE, SO LONG AS YOU ARE BESIDE ME.
IN TIME, THEY CAME TO WHAT WAS SURELY THE PORTAL TO MUSPELHEIM.
YOU'RE TIRED, BALDR--YOUR EYES ARE BLOODSHOT.
THE BATTLE DID YOU NO GOOD, BUT YOU LOOK WORSE THAN EVER.
I ADMIT I'VE FELT BETTER.
BUT FOR EYSA, FOR SVARTALFHEIM, AND FOR ASGARD--
YES, OF COURSE.
IF EYSA HAD KNOWN YOU AS I DO, SHE'D HAVE REALIZED HER WARNING WOULD DRIVE YOU STRAIGHT TO SURTR.
THERE THEY WAITED.
UNTIL...
LOOK!

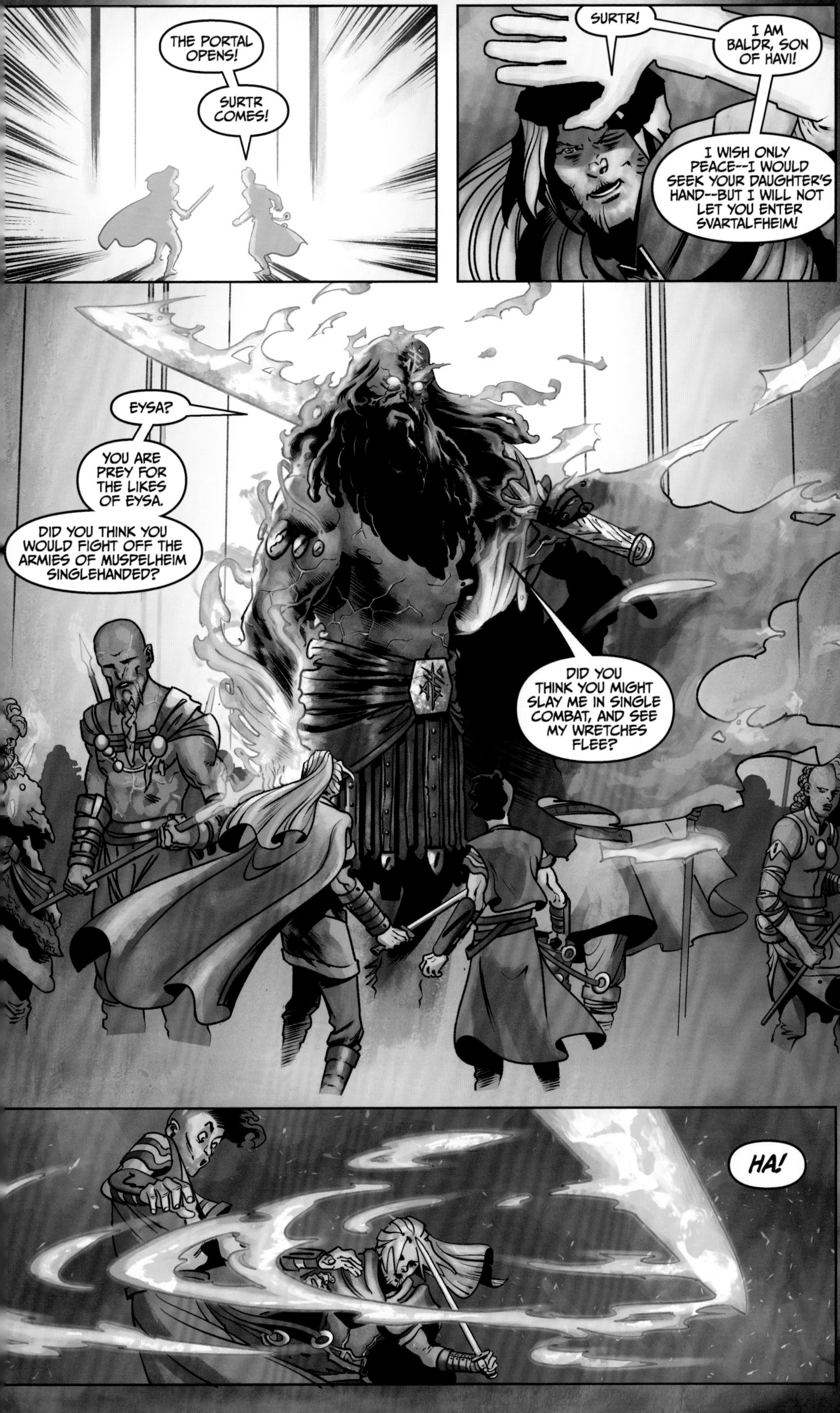
THE PORTAL OPENS!
SURTR COMES!
SURTR!
I AM BALDR, SON OF HAVI!
I WISH ONLY PEACE--I WOULD SEEK YOUR DAUGHTER'S HAND--BUT I WILL NOT LET YOU ENTER SVARTALFHEIM!
EYSA?
YOU ARE PREY FOR THE LIKES OF EYSA.
DID YOU THINK YOU WOULD FIGHT OFF THE ARMIES OF MUSPELHEIM SINGLEHANDED?
DID YOU THINK YOU MIGHT SLAY ME IN SINGLE COMBAT, AND SEE MY WRETCHES FLEE?
HA!

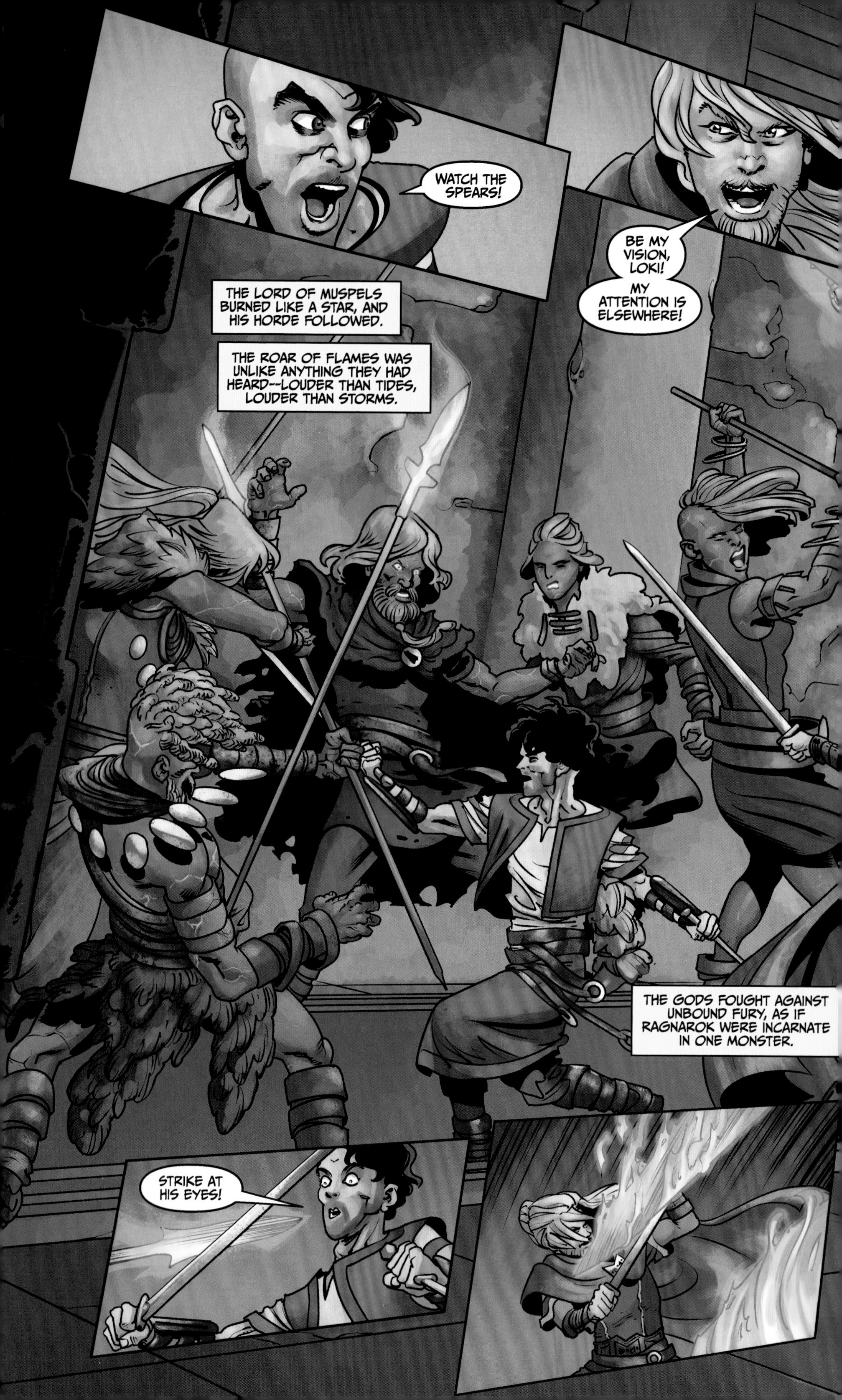
WATCH THE SPEARS!
BE MY VISION, LOKI!
MY ATTENTION IS ELSEWHERE!
THE LORD OF MUSPELS BURNED LIKE A STAR, AND HIS HORDE FOLLOWED.
THE ROAR OF FLAMES WAS UNLIKE ANYTHING THEY HAD HEARD--LOUDER THAN TIDES, LOUDER THAN STORMS.
THE GODS FOUGHT AGAINST UNBOUND FURY, AS IF RAGNAROK WERE INCARNATE IN ONE MONSTER.
STRIKE AT HIS EYES!

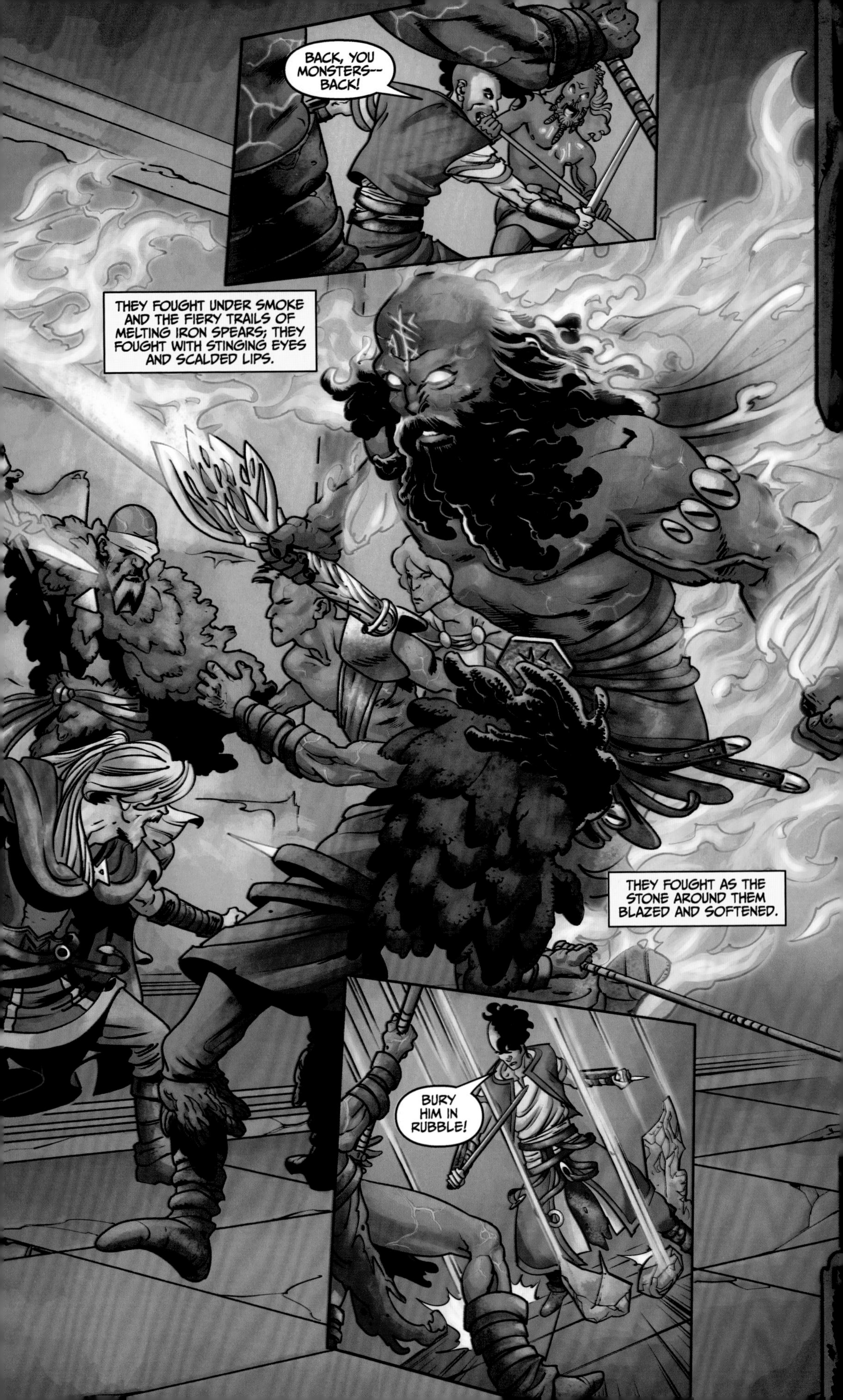
BACK, YOU MONSTERS-- BACK!
THEY FOUGHT UNDER SMOKE AND THE FIERY TRAILS OF MELTING IRON SPEARS; THEY FOUGHT WITH STINGING EYES AND SCALDED LIPS.
THEY FOUGHT AS THE STONE AROUND THEM BLAZED AND SOFTENED.
BURY HIM IN RUBBLE!

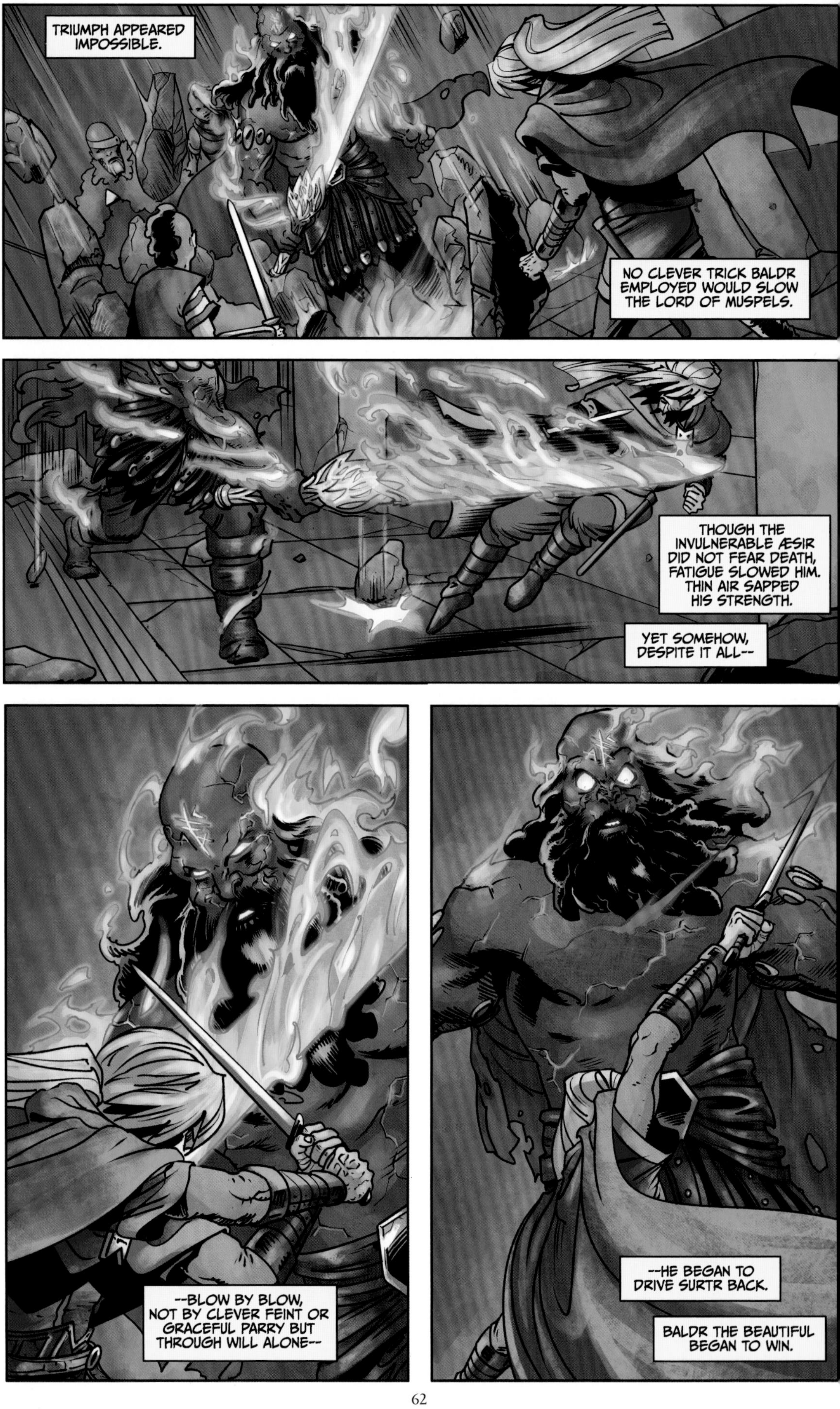
TRIUMPH APPEARED IMPOSSIBLE.
NO CLEVER TRICK BALDR EMPLOYED WOULD SLOW THE LORD OF MUSPELS.
THOUGH THE INVULNERABLE ÆSIR DID NOT FEAR DEATH, FATIGUE SLOWED HIM. THIN AIR SAPPED HIS STRENGTH.
YET SOMEHOW, DESPITE IT ALL--
--BLOW BY BLOW, NOT BY CLEVER FEINT OR GRACEFUL PARRY BUT THROUGH WILL ALONE--
--HE BEGAN TO DRIVE SURTR BACK.
BALDR THE BEAUTIFUL BEGAN TO WIN.

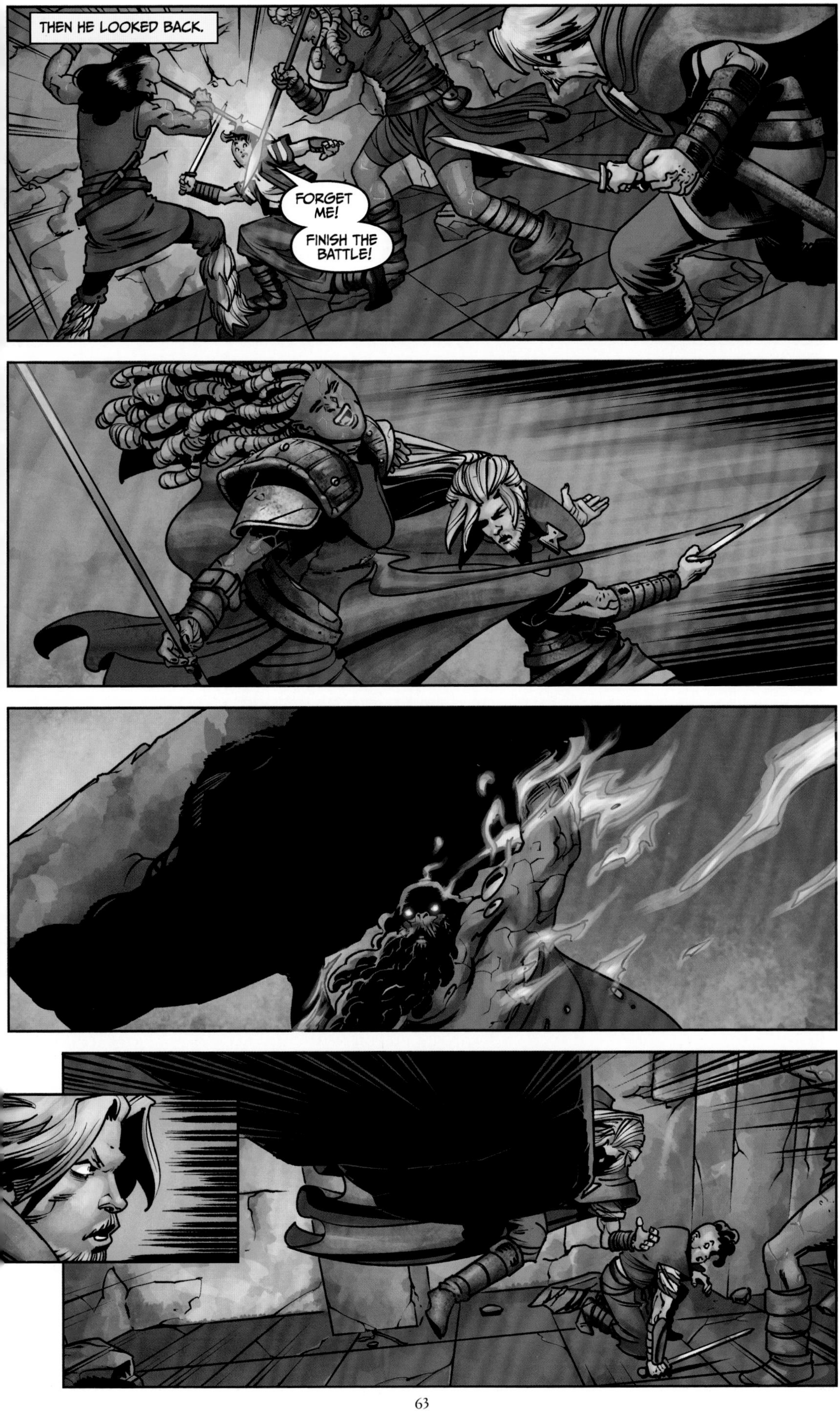
THEN HE LOOKED BACK.
FORGET ME!
FINISH THE BATTLE!

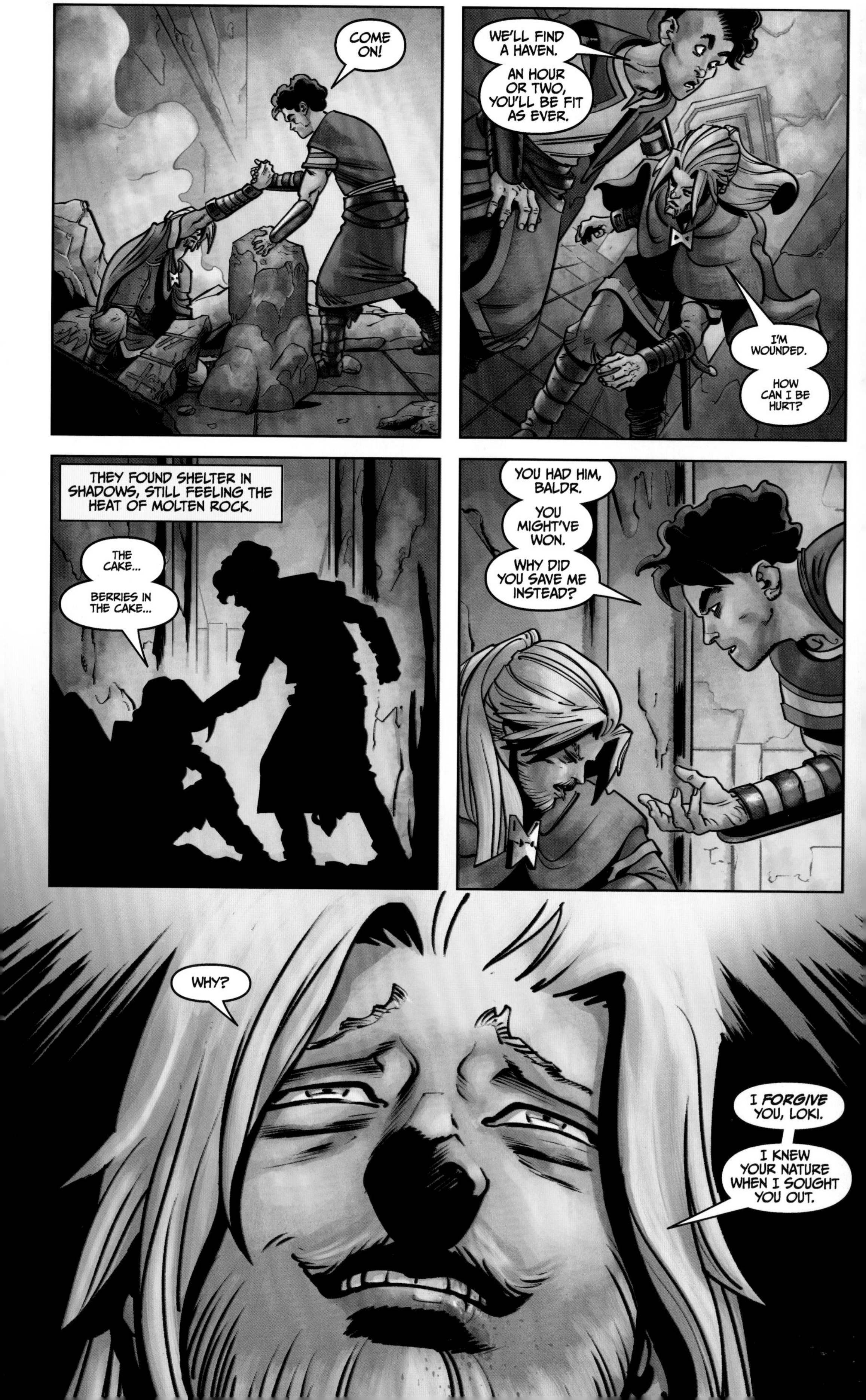
COME ON!
WE'LL FIND A HAVEN.
AN HOUR OR TWO, YOU'LL BE FIT AS EVER.
I'M WOUNDED.
HOW CAN I BE HURT?
THEY FOUND SHELTER IN SHADOWS, STILL FEELING THE HEAT OF MOLTEN ROCK.
THE CAKE...
BERRIES IN THE CAKE...
YOU HAD HIM, BALDR.
YOU MIGHT'VE WON.
WHY DID YOU SAVE ME INSTEAD?
WHY?
I *FORGIVE* YOU, LOKI.
I KNEW YOUR NATURE WHEN I SOUGHT YOU OUT.

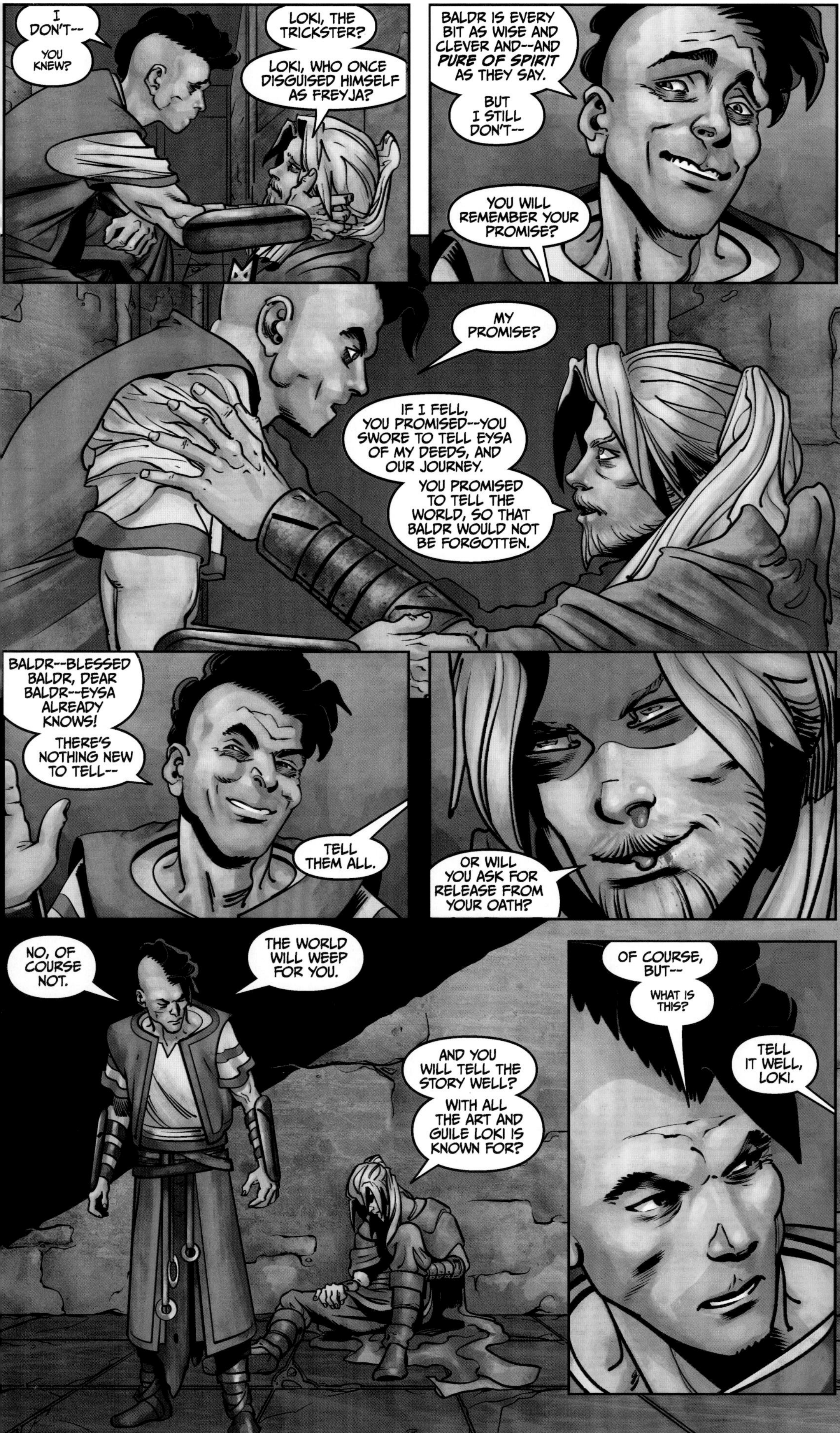
I DON'T--
YOU KNEW?
LOKI, THE TRICKSTER?
LOKI, WHO ONCE DISGUISED HIMSELF AS FREYJA?
BALDR IS EVERY BIT AS WISE AND CLEVER AND--AND *PURE OF SPIRIT* AS THEY SAY.
BUT I STILL DON'T--
YOU WILL REMEMBER YOUR PROMISE?
MY PROMISE?
IF I FELL, YOU PROMISED--YOU SWORE TO TELL EYSA OF MY DEEDS, AND OUR JOURNEY.
YOU PROMISED TO TELL THE WORLD, SO THAT BALDR WOULD NOT BE FORGOTTEN.
BALDR--BLESSED BALDR, DEAR BALDR--EYSA ALREADY KNOWS!
THERE'S NOTHING NEW TO TELL--
TELL THEM ALL.
OR WILL YOU ASK FOR RELEASE FROM YOUR OATH?
NO, OF COURSE NOT.
THE WORLD WILL WEEP FOR YOU.
AND YOU WILL TELL THE STORY WELL?
WITH ALL THE ART AND GUILE LOKI IS KNOWN FOR?
OF COURSE, BUT--
WHAT IS THIS?
TELL IT WELL, LOKI.

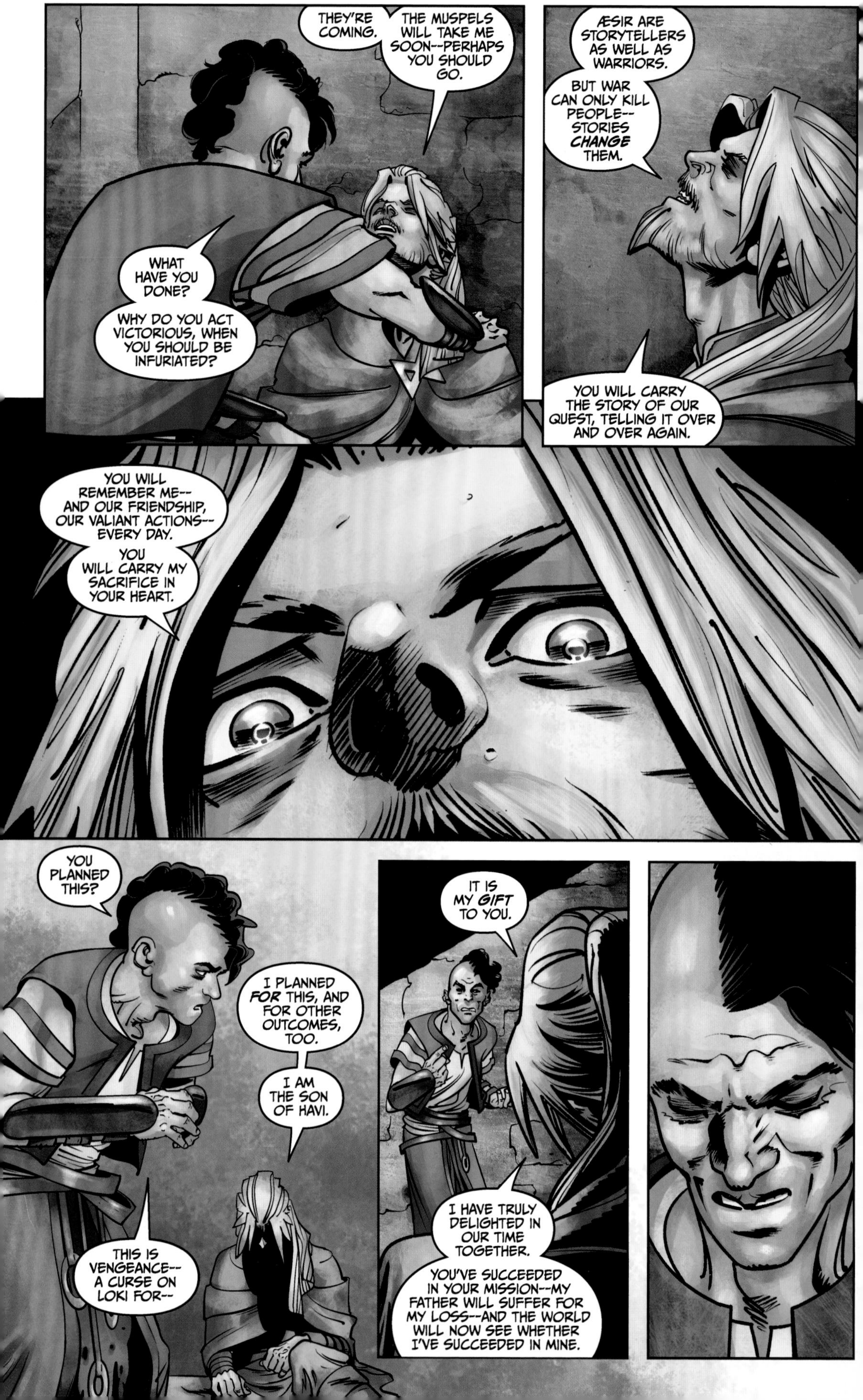

THEY'RE COMING.
THE MUSPELS WILL TAKE ME SOON--PERHAPS YOU SHOULD GO.
WHAT HAVE YOU DONE?
WHY DO YOU ACT VICTORIOUS, WHEN YOU SHOULD BE INFURIATED?
ÆSIR ARE STORYTELLERS AS WELL AS WARRIORS.
BUT WAR CAN ONLY KILL PEOPLE--STORIES CHANGE THEM.
YOU WILL CARRY THE STORY OF OUR QUEST, TELLING IT OVER AND OVER AGAIN.
YOU WILL REMEMBER ME--AND OUR FRIENDSHIP, OUR VALIANT ACTIONS--EVERY DAY.
YOU WILL CARRY MY SACRIFICE IN YOUR HEART.
YOU PLANNED THIS?
I PLANNED FOR THIS, AND FOR OTHER OUTCOMES, TOO.
I AM THE SON OF HAVI.
THIS IS VENGEANCE--A CURSE ON LOKI FOR--
IT IS MY GIFT TO YOU.
I HAVE TRULY DELIGHTED IN OUR TIME TOGETHER.
YOU'VE SUCCEEDED IN YOUR MISSION--MY FATHER WILL SUFFER FOR MY LOSS--AND THE WORLD WILL NOW SEE WHETHER I'VE SUCCEEDED IN MINE.

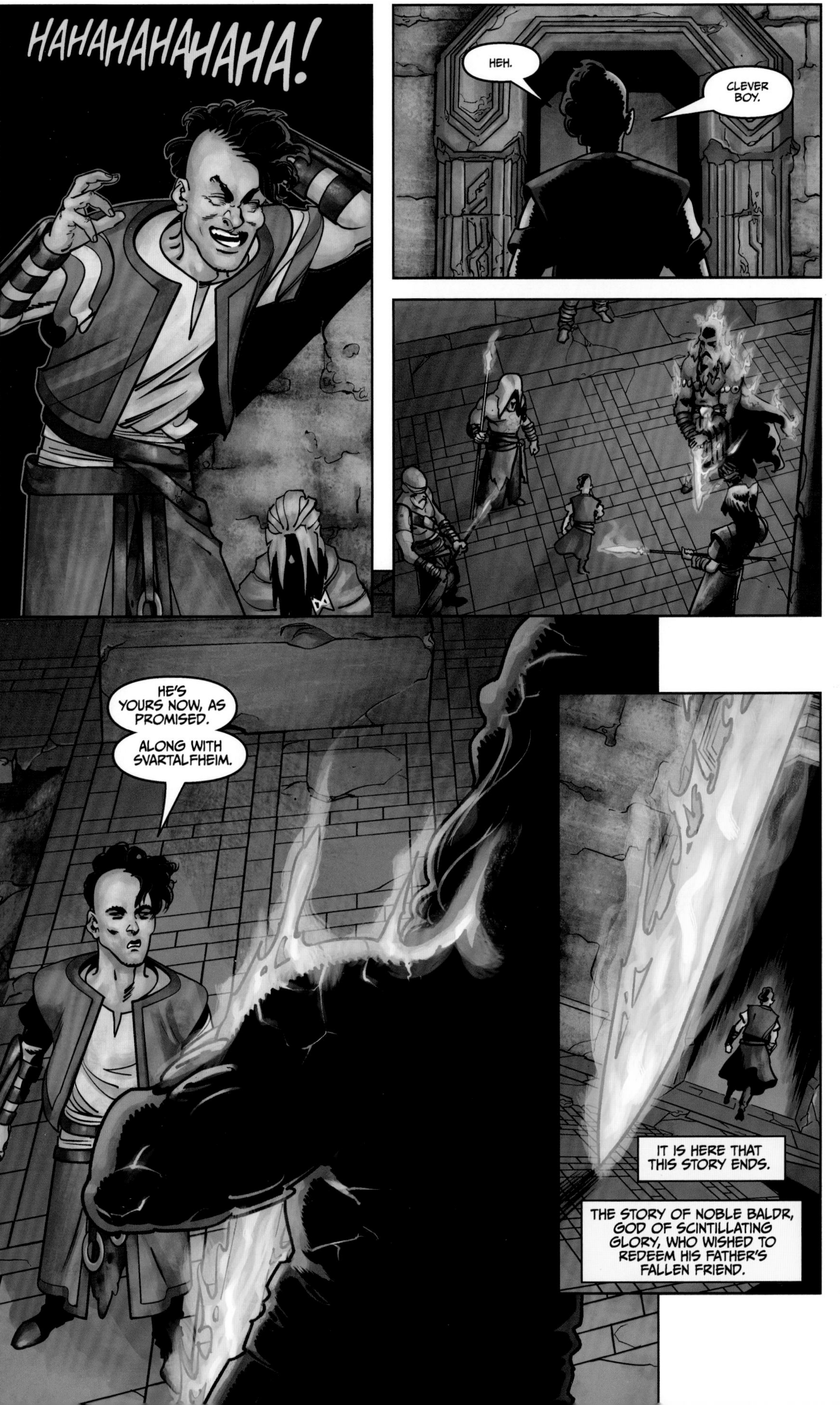
HAHAHAHAHAHAHA!
HEH.
CLEVER BOY.
HE'S YOURS NOW, AS PROMISED.
ALONG WITH SVARTALFHEIM.
IT IS HERE THAT THIS STORY ENDS.
THE STORY OF NOBLE BALDR, GOD OF SCINTILLATING GLORY, WHO WISHED TO REDEEM HIS FATHER'S FALLEN FRIEND.

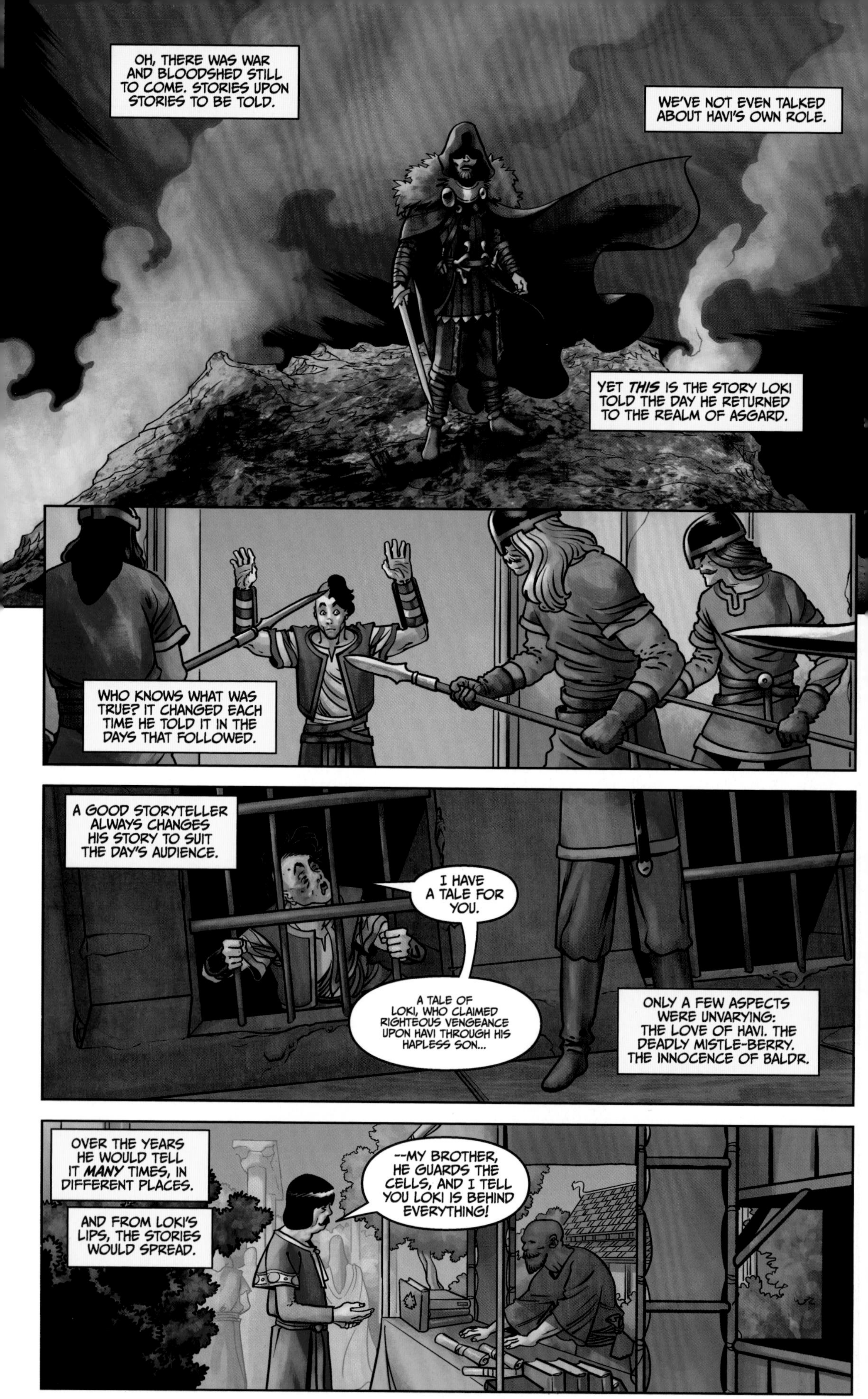

OH, THERE WAS WAR AND BLOODSHED STILL TO COME. STORIES UPON STORIES TO BE TOLD.
WE'VE NOT EVEN TALKED ABOUT HAVI'S OWN ROLE.
YET *THIS* IS THE STORY LOKI TOLD THE DAY HE RETURNED TO THE REALM OF ASGARD.
WHO KNOWS WHAT WAS TRUE? IT CHANGED EACH TIME HE TOLD IT IN THE DAYS THAT FOLLOWED.
A GOOD STORYTELLER ALWAYS CHANGES HIS STORY TO SUIT THE DAY'S AUDIENCE.
I HAVE A TALE FOR YOU.
A TALE OF LOKI, WHO CLAIMED RIGHTEOUS VENGEANCE UPON HAVI THROUGH HIS HAPLESS SON...
ONLY A FEW ASPECTS WERE UNVARYING: THE LOVE OF HAVI. THE DEADLY MISTLE-BERRY. THE INNOCENCE OF BALDR.
OVER THE YEARS HE WOULD TELL IT *MANY* TIMES, IN DIFFERENT PLACES.
AND FROM LOKI'S LIPS, THE STORIES WOULD SPREAD.
--MY BROTHER, HE GUARDS THE CELLS, AND I TELL YOU LOKI IS BEHIND EVERYTHING!

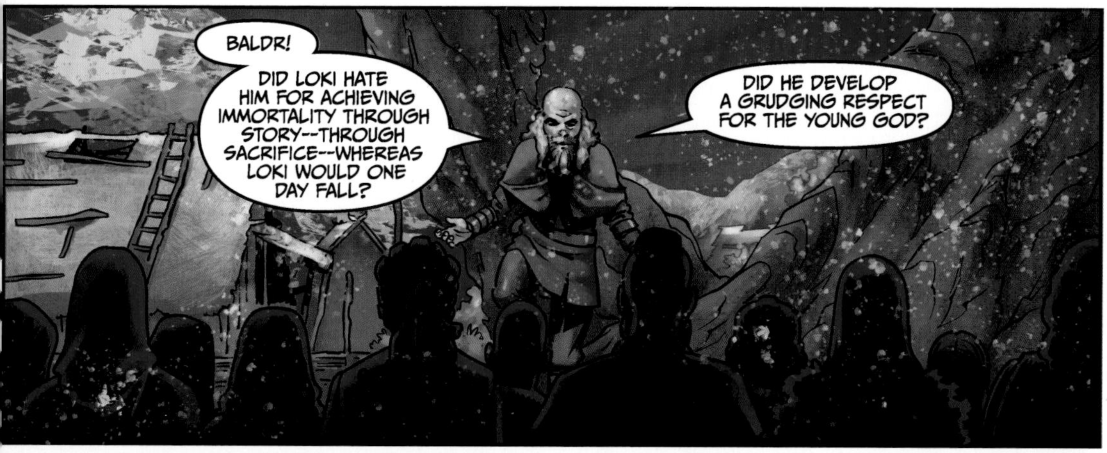
BALDR!
DID LOKI HATE HIM FOR ACHIEVING IMMORTALITY THROUGH STORY--THROUGH SACRIFICE--WHEREAS LOKI WOULD ONE DAY FALL?
DID HE DEVELOP A GRUDGING RESPECT FOR THE YOUNG GOD?

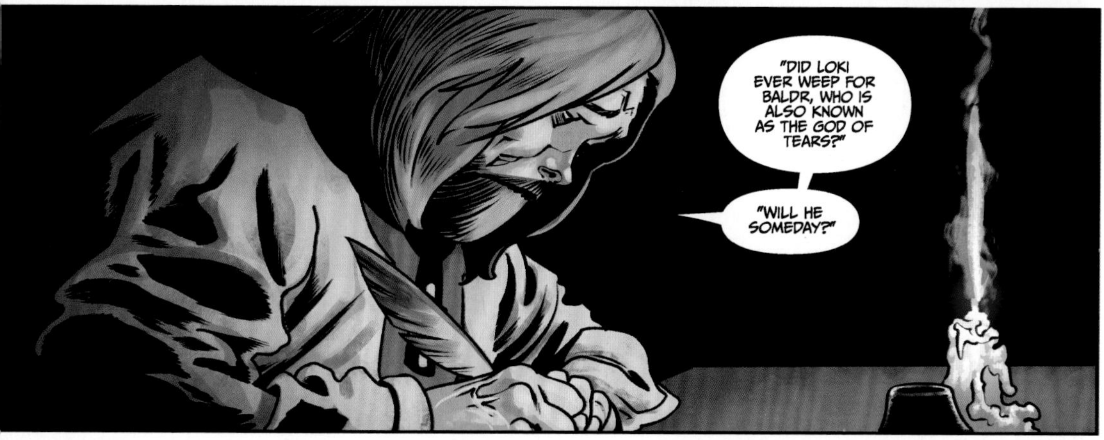
"DID LOKI EVER WEEP FOR BALDR, WHO IS ALSO KNOWN AS THE GOD OF TEARS?"
"WILL HE SOMEDAY?"

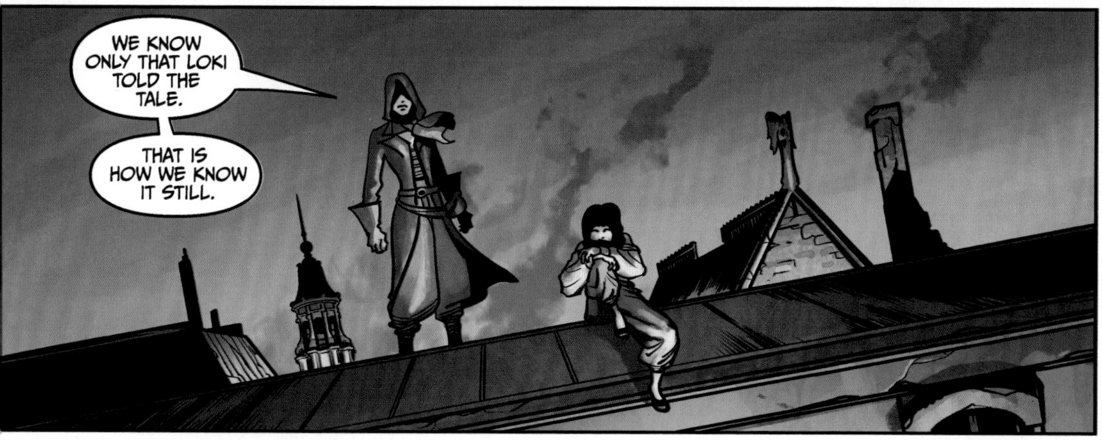
WE KNOW ONLY THAT LOKI TOLD THE TALE.
THAT IS HOW WE KNOW IT STILL.

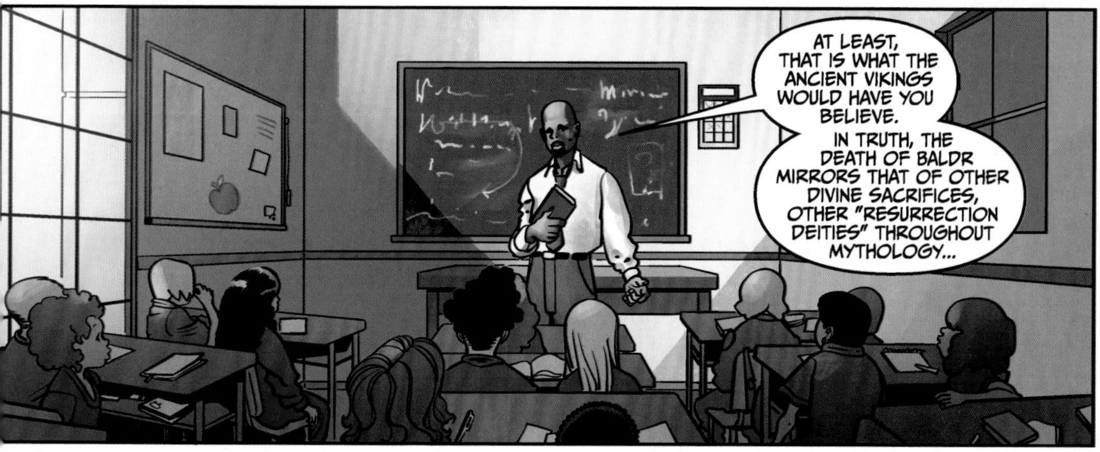
AT LEAST, THAT IS WHAT THE ANCIENT VIKINGS WOULD HAVE YOU BELIEVE.
IN TRUTH, THE DEATH OF BALDR MIRRORS THAT OF OTHER DIVINE SACRIFICES, OTHER "RESURRECTION DEITIES" THROUGHOUT MYTHOLOGY...

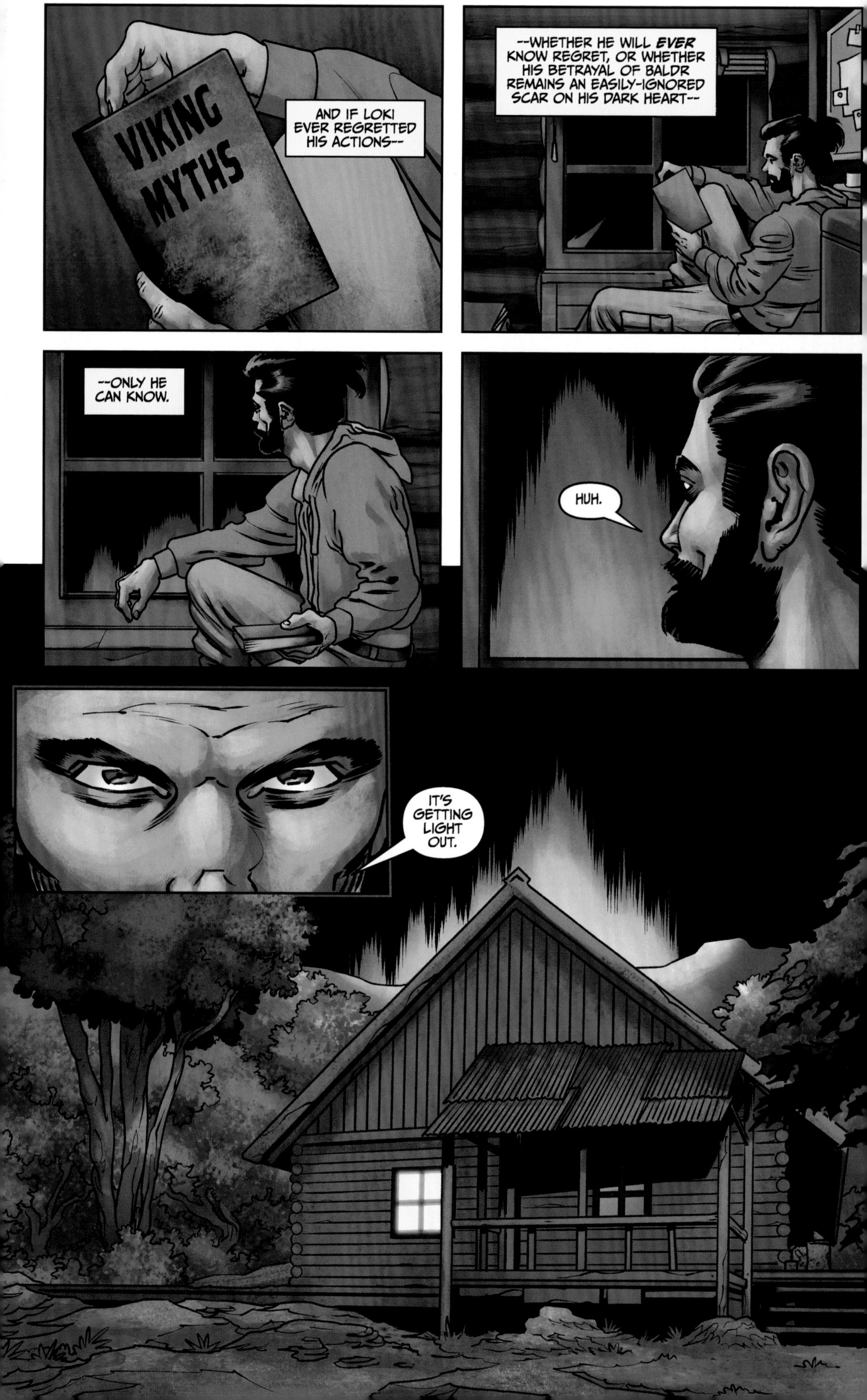
VIKING MYTHS
AND IF LOKI EVER REGRETTED HIS ACTIONS--
--WHETHER HE WILL EVER KNOW REGRET, OR WHETHER HIS BETRAYAL OF BALDR REMAINS AN EASILY-IGNORED SCAR ON HIS DARK HEART--
--ONLY HE CAN KNOW.
HUH.
IT'S GETTING LIGHT OUT.

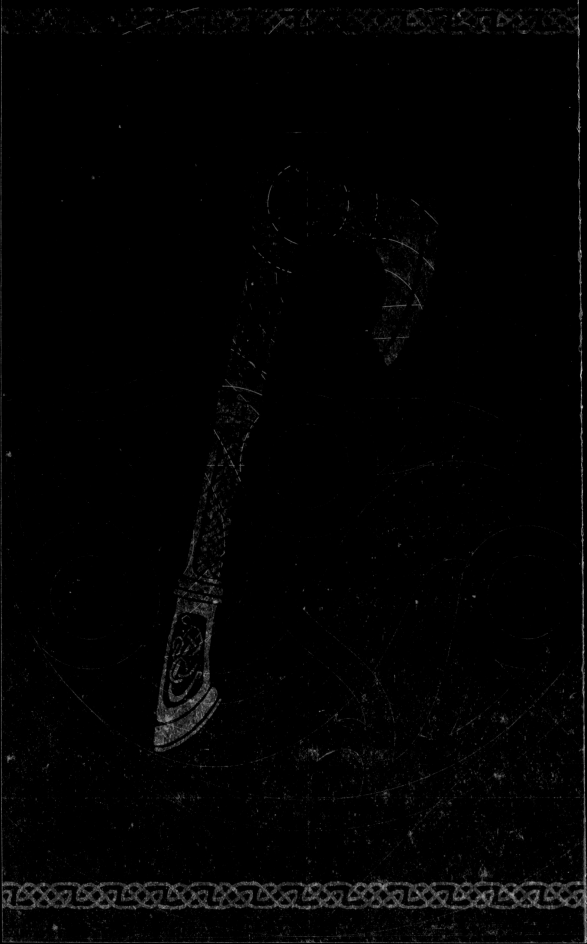